● **Reclaiming the Ministry
of All God's People**

Total
Ministry

Stewart C. Zabriskie

An Alban Institute Publication

The Publications Program of The Alban Institute is assisted by a grant from
Trinity Church, New York City.

Library of Congress Catalog Card Number 95-78602
ISBN 1-56699-155-2

CONTENTS

FOREWORD

Stewart Zabriskie is a pioneer: this book is about the frontiers of ministry in today's churches.

No issues are more troubling to church leaders today than the one Zabriskie addresses here: **What is to be the shape of leadership in the church of tomorrow, and how do we make it happen?**

The traditional answer common to the denominations has been that leadership is a professional function and is primarily to be provided by seminary-trained persons in a variety of roles (Zabriskie, an Episcopalian, uses the terms of his church: "bishop, priest, and deacon"). The traditional answer probably served the church well a generation ago, but it does not serve the world or the task of ministry we face as we move into the 21st century.

The churches cling to the traditional pattern, with seminary-trained leaders at all levels because those patterns *are* traditional, they are familiar, they do have important values, and also because they are very, very hard to change. Indeed, since the second World War, a number of denominations that previously welcomed other kinds of leadership (The Church of the Brethren, The United Methodist Church, etc.) moved strongly toward replacing nonprofessional church leaders with professionals.

In more recent years, however, as financial pressure on the churches has grown, increasing discomfort with our single-minded reliance on professional clergy has surfaced everywhere. Very small congregations simply cannot afford to pay what it costs to support a full-time professionally trained clergyperson. That pragmatic concern for paying the bills may have had a role in turning people's minds toward alternative leadership models during the past generation, but Zabriskie, and the

Episcopal Diocese of Nevada of which he is bishop, is a pioneer for a much larger concern.

In the book he describes a pioneering model—"Total Ministry." It is a vision of the ministry of the whole people of God in which ministries of all members are integrated with one another and in which leadership is a function of the whole body. The purpose of total ministry is to have every member of the church fully engaged in serving the world, while those with special skills are identified to help do those things that the institution needs to have done to provide the support for the body.

Within that vision, the traditional roles are indeed lived out differently. Zabriskie tells you about some of the people who are living those roles differently: Dale, who is a pharmacist-priest; Madge, a dry-goods store manager who doubles as local priest. He tells about the diaconal ministry of Bonnie in jails and community service, and he tells about Burt, a pediatrician who also serves as priest. And there are others.

As he describes how the vision is operating in the towns of Nevada, you begin to see how the pragmatic concerns are there, but are not the motivating factors. This is an attempt to discover better ministries, more ministries, fuller lives of service, not a cheaper method of parish administration.

There is much less dependence upon the professional leadership of clergy, much more on the functions of leadership needed to do what we have relied upon clergy to do in the past. The model affects how laity carry out their ministries, how ordained persons in the diocese carry out their ministries, and even how the bishop carries out his ministry. His chapter on learning to let go of control should be "must" reading for those in judicatory roles.

I happen to know that Zabriskie is also pioneering in another substantial way. He acknowledges building on foundations others have laid in a time when most judicatory executives, bishops, and clergy I know seem to feel that the only way to affirm their own leadership is to invent a new "vision" that puts their own personal stamp upon their leadership. It is refreshing to see someone talking about servant leadership and ministry who also walks the walk.

Loren B. Mead

ACKNOWLEDGMENTS

I thank the people who are the church in Nevada for including me in their adventure and allowing me to listen and to learn with them. My thanks also go to Celia Hahn for her wise and helpful counsel as this book developed, to editor Evelyn Bence for her careful directions, and to my secretary, Martha Brooks, whose computer literacy has saved me untold hours of work.

Special gratitude goes to Howard Anderson who in Minnesota some years ago introduced me to the new vistas of total ministry without telling me what he was doing! While there are many others to thank, none is as profoundly important as my wife, Sarah, whose patience, encouragement, and support help to keep the vision alive.

INTRODUCTION

Some years ago I lived and worked in suburban Minneapolis. It was a growing residential area, and commercial establishments were eager to search out new customers. Most any occasion, it seemed, a new or used car sale, the opening of a shopping mall, a new crafts boutique, was frequently marked by rented search lights sweeping the suburban heavens with beckoning beams. I suppose the principle was something akin to following a rainbow to its end. Consumed by curiosity or a need for adventure, the potential shopper would spy the beams in the sky and search out their origin, there to find a Great Deal. Of course one could resist the exploration; sitting back and watching those great beams of light dance in the sky did provide a simple pleasure of its own.

A young friend in the parish gave another context to those lights. Ben was four or five years old at the time, and one evening he turned to his mother and shared his vision: "They're looking for angels!"

I can think of no better way to describe personal involvement in the adventure we call "total ministry." It is an avenue into meeting and discovering angels hard at work being God's servants in the most ordinary places and in the most commonplace ways. In both Old and New Testaments, as well as in continuing human experience, angels express or announce the presence of God in life. Of course there is always the extraordinary standout here and there, the archangel or notable saint, but the ministering angels, or the communion of saints, to recall a worthy phrase, often catch us unaware and call us anew into the possibilities of the ordinary in Christian ministry—total Christian ministry.

What do I mean by *total ministry*? The increasingly widespread and popular term describes the shared ministry of all baptized people. In many of its applications, total ministry moves away from a primary focus on the ministry of the ordained and includes the laity in the mutual work of ministry. There is *one* ministry in Christ and all baptized people—lay and ordained—participate in it according to the gifts given them.

Different places and people approach that understanding in a variety of ways and with different emphases. While that diversity may seem to contribute to some of the confusion about what *total ministry* means and how it is worked out in the life of today's church, that variety also represents quite accurately the rich texture of the church's whole (or total) ministry: what we are learning to celebrate as the church's continuing and inspired diversity, which seems to be part of its unity in the Spirit.

No long history of total ministry need appear here, but we need to remember two bishops who opened the doors to this new but old expression of Christian ministry: The Rt. Rev. William Gordon, bishop of Alaska from 1948 to 1974 and The Rt. Rev. Wesley Frensdorff, bishop of Nevada from 1972 to 1985. These two called upon the work of Roland Allen, an Anglican missionary to North China from 1895 to 1903.[1] Allen's writings about his sense of mission among indigenous peoples reminded the church of its New Testament roots in ministry, with special insight into the value of local, indigenous ministries.

In Alaska Gordon began the process of training and ordaining local elders for priesthood in villages that were accessible only by sled or small airplane. No one knows how many conversations, communications, and explorations Gordon and Frensdorff had before Gordon came to a Nevada clergy conference in 1974, where he told the clergy and also the diocesan council about his experience in Alaska. Like Alaska to some extent, Nevada has a number of small remote churches that could not afford to pay full-time priests, nor did the diocese subsidize their acquisition of full-time clergy. In the context of Gordon's seminal experience and subsequent reflection and conversation in Nevada, a new vision for ministry development began to emerge.

This was not an easy birth—of new understandings and expressions of ministry.[2] Enthusiasm and energy for change are often greeted by wariness and resistance.

For far too long "ministry" had meant "clergy"; "minister" had referred to an ordained person. Most congregations newly led by lay ministers felt a corresponding sense of loss coupled with a vestigial hope for "when we have a minister again."

The reality of economics became a spiritual nutrient in the educational process developed by Frensdorff and his staff to prepare congregations for the ministry of all the baptized, even for functions traditionally served by ordained clergy. Bishop and staff traveled the vastness of Nevada's mountains and deserts to teach appropriate biblical study, to access and affirm gifts through discovery workshops, and to develop a process for the calling and ordination of "local" clergy, who would be called and trained to serve only in the parish in which they lived in order to keep alive the sacramental life of the congregation.

Some people were confused at first. Some dropped out of regular participation. Others caught the enthusiasm and the "experiment" became a journey. And in that process, doors that once had led *into* church became swinging doors. Ecclesiological windows were cleaned and even stained glass theology became transparent with the vision of a church that not only gathered, but also went *out* in the presence and actions of all its members.

I add here what is perhaps only a paraphrase of what others have noted about this early work in total ministry. The significance of Bill Gordon's and Wes Frensdorff's work was not that they created a new system, but that they were theologically radical in the sense of being deeply rooted. They began a process of theological and spiritual exploration that has challenged our structures and our special conceits and contentments. They did not close doors, but struggled to open them wider and to throw open some windows as well, so that the Christian household could welcome the presence of the Lord of ministry and venture out in his presence. The genius was not to have a "Gordon model" or a "Frensdorff model," but to have an honest theological and spiritual foundation for responding to the continuing work of the Spirit in ministry.

There is a true story I have enjoyed telling on a number of occasions and in as many contexts. It seems appropriate here as something of an explanation of the response our forebears in total ministry are calling us to continue exploring. This incident occurred during my senior year at the General Theological Seminary in New York City. I was doing Sunday field work across the Hudson River at Trinity Cathedral in Newark, New Jersey. A part of that job was the superintendency of the small Sunday morning church school that gathered in the diocesan cathedral house down the street.

In early October the inevitable seasonal question was raised: "Should we have a Christmas pageant this year?"

The unanimous and almost immediate response from the church school teachers was no! "You never know who is going to show up, and Mary always gets sick at the last moment." In consultation with the dean, I proposed what seemed a fair alternative. We would have an early Epiphany party sometime in the twelve days of Christmas, a time when most parents would be eager to encourage their children's attendance. In the context of that party, we would try to convey to the children the energy and the momentum of the magi's trip to Bethlehem.

We had a wonderful physical plant to work with and "journey through": several floors with stairwells, a variety of offices, a gymnasium, and a lovely little chapel on the main floor which would serve as an ideal manger for the climax of the journey.

Preparations went well, and when the day arrived I felt assured that we would be in for a fine "trip." Everything seemed in good order. Three high school students were somewhat grudgingly attired in someone's old drapes, representing the three magi. Ahead of them an acolyte was bearing an aluminum foil star on a long stick, a ready guide. Behind them, the children were lined up, and an air of general excitement filled the main floor auditorium where the trip would begin. The only thing I had forgotten was a doll for Mary to hold, but I showed her how to hold her arms so that it would appear she was holding an infant.

We set out on our journey. Upstairs and down, over hills and through valleys. Suddenly out of a second floor room burst some junior high shepherds, filled with the excitement and wonder of what they had seen in Bethlehem. Proceeding on to the gymnasium in the basement, we found ourselves in Herod's court. Herod was a fellow seminarian with a beard, and he and his advisors were poring over some antique–looking maps I had made up earlier that week. Herod looked up from the maps. With just the right note of menace in his voice, he asked them to be sure and come back and tell him where this child was, so that he could go and find him, too.

The great moment finally arrived as the procession drew near the little chapel. Everything was in good order. The candles were lit. Mary was kneeling at the opening in the altar rail just as I had instructed, and Joseph was standing somewhat woodenly behind her, but he was there! It was a beautiful tableau, and the children crowded eagerly into the chapel to be part of it. I stood at the entrance and gazed proudly at the scene—the results of my efforts.

But my self-congratulatory reverie was interrupted by noises I had not planned. "Where's the baby? Where's the baby Jesus? We can't *see* the baby Jesus!" as the children craned forward to see the object of their journey. At that point, our teen-aged Joseph came to life and announced in a clear New Jersey accent, "There ain't no baby!"

And being warned of God in a dream, the wise men departed into their own country by another way.

After some time of recovery and reflection, I realized that Joseph was right. There ain't no baby. And there ain't a lot more, too. There ain't any longer that beautiful person walking in our midst to teach, to touch, to listen, and to heal. There ain't the dying Savior hanging on the cross as a visible sign of sacrificial love. There ain't the concrete if startling vision of the risen Lord outside the empty tomb, or the intensity of rushing wind and tongues of fire to move us into bold ministry. These are the wonderful pictures, the deep roots and truths of our faith, and they are at the heart of our gallery of faithful pictures. But the very story those pictures recall asks for more than memory. It shows us that there is room for more pictures in the same gallery, pictures of other people, ordinary and extraordinary, who continue the story in a contemporariness of Spirit that is exciting and alive. It is a picture of ministry that requires personal immediacy in the sense of presence; we are dealing with more than a "you were there" kind of story. We are living a "he is here!" story.

When a story is related there often is a storyteller and there are the listeners; or there is a pageant and those who come to watch it. Total ministry approaches the story in a different way. Total ministry acknowledges that every baptized Christian is a storyteller by being a story-liver—one who lives the story—with a lifestyle outlined well in the baptismal covenant as found in the Episcopal *Book of Common Prayer*. The "He is here!" story is told in our profession of belief (creed) and in our gathering for insight, communion, sacrament, and prayer. It is told in a conduct responsive to the good in life and a conduct repentant for our attraction to the destructive in life; in our commitment to the good news of God in Christ rather than the bad news so rampant in our cultures and societies; in our vision of a Christ present among others, together with a respect for each one's dignity that encourages our struggle for justice and peace. The story is written daily by those in whom Christ works daily, his ministers, who are all the baptized. There ain't no baby. There is so much more. There is *we*, as body or household or community or church or whatever other timely description one might choose.

Baptismal covenant, as seen by our forebears in total ministry, opens up the scope of ministry, throws the doors and windows of Christian work and experience wide open: not as a denial of tradition but as a way of enabling that tradition to be accountable and truly "handed over" so that the "He is here!" story can happen in his ministers. For tradition, rightly understood, is far more than past history, though it preserves for us the story of the God of history at work in history. Tradition is also the way in which the present receives that past and, guided by the Spirit, presses on to the future, with something of the vision that the apostle Paul shared with the Philippians (Phil. 3:12-16), putting behind a captivity to past experience only by remaining open to new visions or "words" from God.

In these pages it is my intention to revisit that sense of healthy tradition-with-momentum as it is expressed in the development of total ministry. Much of my experience comes from learning with the people in the Diocese of Nevada, and I shall call upon that experience to provide specific examples of a shape and direction that total ministry can take. I have also had the privilege of sharing some insights with lay and ordained people in other dioceses who continue to contribute to the vision of an emerging ministry in Christ's church. And I owe much to the people of the church in Aotearoa, New Zealand, and Polynesia; some have visited us in Nevada, and many welcomed us into their parishes. Their questions, their hopes, and the exciting vision they have of a ministering community—multicultural and respectful of and even reverent about diversity, with a willingness to sacrifice some of what is past to face with a holy fear what God's future might bring—has been inspiring grist for the total-ministry mill.

And holy fear is one of the underpinnings of the adventure in total ministry. For it is about repentance, or a willingness to change, so that God's reign might be more clearly expressed than we have seen; and change, even if it is called repentance, is a scary thing. It is about openness or humility: a posture of being vulnerable to the Holy Spirit to the extent that we mean the prayer "thy will be done," even if it does change the structures with which we have become content. And it is about being foolish enough to press on anyway, knowing that mistakes will happen, being assured that such foolishness can be wiser than the kind of control that keeps everything safely in place.

In my Nevada office I've hung a picture of a ship that has this inscription: "A ship is safe in a harbor, but that's not what a ship is for." That has a peculiar relevance in this diocese of deserts and mountains, and it is part of what prompts this attempt to revisit the bases of total ministry, to see where we may have strayed and, even more important, where we are being led.

Before I was elected bishop here in Nevada, I had a pretty clear idea of what bishops—that is, *others* with that responsibility—should do. That perspective was altered almost immediately when I actually became a bishop—perhaps testimony to a particular grace in that ordination! I discovered that if I was to be part of the ministry of all the baptized in this diocese, I needed to listen to them first. So I spent the first year or so mostly listening, not only to an "inner circle" of a staff that had some initial difficulty including me, but also to people in congregations who were excited, confused, looking ahead, worried, some even hoping that I would turn the clock back to the good old days when "we had a real minister." In that listening exercise I learned anew the importance of Jesus' example in the Gospel of Luke as he set his face to journey to Jerusalem (Luke 9:51ff). The following chapters in Luke's account attest to Jesus' flexibility as he turned aside again and again to listen or heal or teach—to pay attention to those along the way who perhaps gave deep context to the sacrifice he was going to make.

In 1986 when I was being interviewed as part of Nevada's search for a bishop, someone asked me, "Are you the kind of leader who rushes ahead without looking back to see if anyone is following?" The message was clear. We are being led together as a ministering community, and the discernment of the Spirit's direction is community business in which we all share.

And listening is not just a job for the leadership, but it is one for the entire community. The mistakes happen when we do not listen to one another and become fond of "innovative" ideas that stand too much by themselves. We listen instead to how the Spirit speaks to and among us. So the pages that follow are about hope, a dangerous hope perhaps, because it allows the Holy Spirit to interrupt some of our preoccupations and comfort zones and lead us into risky adventure.

CHAPTER 1

Total Ministry
and Model-Based Ministry

The imagery for total ministry moves away from the hierarchical and pyramidal structures into images that suggest mutuality, equality of order, the sharing of gifts and energy in and as community. And such imagery derives from the conviction that the systemic nature of the church is generated and expressed by the Holy Spirit in our midst.

Total ministry, or the recognition of the ministry of all the baptized, is as old as the New Testament and as "new" as these last few decades of the twentieth century. As noted previously in the introduction, its emergence in the Alaska and Nevada Episcopal dioceses twenty-five years ago signaled something of a radical reassessment of the church's way of living into and living out Christian ministry and mission, with special concern for small churches in remote areas and circumstances. As with any kind of radical or "rooted" change, this new adventure met with some surprise, some interest, and some resistance.

In the course of that early exploration, the bishop of Alaska, Bill Gordon, worked on the development of a canon or church law that would provide for the calling, training, and ordination of "local clergy"—people who would be called from within their own congregations in remote places to serve in those congregations only; its eventual inclusion in the denominational canons or laws (Canon III.8, later renumbered III.9) added a new dimension to the Episcopal Church's governance. (See Appendix 1 for text of canons.)

During the 1970s, when Bishop Wes Frensdorff was leading the Diocese of Nevada in its exploration of the meanings and possibilities of what is now known as *total ministry*. That effort was known simply as the *Nevada Experiment*. Some continued to use that term affectionately, if patronizingly, long after *total ministry* was a working reality in this diocese. Total ministry broke an Episcopal mold, and it served as the occasion for some apprehension especially around the use of the new canon that allowed for the training and ordination of those who would come to be called "local clergy."

Those wedded to models of professional ministry felt some early nervousness about these developments, and some of that attitude still exists in places, especially regarding who may vote in church conventions. Just as forbidding, however, was an enthusiasm to embrace and label this kind of ministry energy as a new system begetting new models for the church. That excitement led to the creation of task forces and committees or commissions that tried to create a new jargon for a new model. When we visited New Zealand in 1992, we were frequently asked to share the "Nevada model."

Each time I had to confess that there is no such thing as a Nevada model, and most certainly not in Nevada; we had no system of models to bring for transplanting in other locales. I explained that indeed we are on a spiritual journey into God's future. We have made some mistakes that we can warn others to avoid, and we have learned some valuable lessons that we happily share. But we have no set of models to sell. Even the language we use to talk about ministry is continually evolving, dodging the eddies of jargon and trying not to contribute to the church's habit of beating certain buzz words to death—among them, unhappily, even the word *ministry*.

Total ministry is not a system as the word is traditionally used. It is the acceptance of an inspiration, and Jesus Christ is the Good News at its center. Around that center a community orbits and moves further into God's outer space—God's future, where Christ is all and in all, that dimension of life and ministry into which God's Spirit would lead us. For as many theologians have noted, God is the God of the future far more than of the past.

I need to clarify my apparently negative use of the word *system*, because I do appreciate the kinds of systemic change to which the church is being called and to which it is responding. But sometimes the church has developed systems, for management and leadership and church growth, for instance, expressed in models that often ignore and obscure the organic or systemic nature of the church. In such a scheme the church becomes more of an organization than an organism. Labels and categories are the outward signs of such systems; a special jargon becomes attached that assumes a special worth-ship for a season or two or three. And so we come up with "models" and "steps-to-take" and "organizing principles" and tendencies to categorize that do from time to time offer some helpful guidelines, but when they get set in concrete, they lose their energy and become "systems" expressing only organizational models. Such systems and models can quickly become transformed into the specters that lament "But we're used to doing it this way!" Whether it's true or not, the lament haunts the households of those who respond to the call for systemic change.

"System" Traps

The story of the Transfiguration in the synoptic gospels helps me clarify my unease about model-based systems. Once Peter, James, and John had witnessed Jesus' glory, their first impulse was to memorialize it, to set up some kind of structure to which they could point and say, "This is what Jesus' story is about." While it is dangerous to impute intentions to the disciples, nonetheless the ensuing verses in each of the three accounts suggest that the disciples were missing the point of what they had witnessed. "This is my Son, the Beloved; listen to him!" (Mark 9:7). And what did Jesus have to say? "He ordered them to tell no one about what they had seen until after the Son of Man had risen from the dead" (v. 9). The creation of a model in whatever shape—buying into an old system of concretizing a moment of vision—would distract from the story and the vision yet to come: The resurrection of Jesus was to be such a revolutionary act that it would regather the pieces of the story up until then into a whole new sense of life's dimensions.

In that pivotal New Testament story, I sense the need for an urgent commitment to the *flow* of God's story, moving us from a traditional need to mark the spot and make models to a posture of listening and waiting for the continuing revelation of God's direction in life.

So I speak of such systems as attempts to make sense out of mystery; they make room for an attendant danger of putting things in place, as in storage or pigeon-holes. They in turn can become the rationale for *keeping* things in place and missing the mystery of how life flows in an organism. For as we look at the systemic nature of the human body or of the body we call church, we cannot deny the core mystery expressed in their genesis and function.

Misunderstandings come from other flanks, too. One visitor to our diocese went home and announced that someone in Nevada had told him that "total ministry" was just another way of keeping dying churches going. It was, he reported, the triumph of maintenance over mission. In one sense he was quite right, and I have needed to reflect on his observation. I think he would agree that the church is always dying in some way if we are doing our job of listening to and following the Lord. And there is something to be said in due course about the relationship of maintenance and mission. Much depends, however, on what picture of "church" one harbors and how dependent that picture may be on old definitions and old models of success and survival. One might even ask a further question of the apparently disenchanted Nevadan who made the initial observation, "What's so bad about restoring life to the dying?"

Spirituality and Mission

Total ministry is rooted in a spirituality that relies heavily on listening: first in prayer to God, and then to one another. And that listening leads inevitably into mission, because that is the job description, the covenant responsibility, of the ministering Christian community. We do not minister alone or as proxy for anyone else; we have company in mission. This root "listening" spirituality results from the response of individual people to the call into the communion of saints—the company—that is at first *centripetal* (it gathers and embraces) and then it is *centrifugal* (it orbits out from and around a gravitational center). It is part of the nature of this community, as it is part of the nature of its Lord, *to attract and to send*. So the ministry of this company—or communion—is always in tension between being center-grounded or center-bearing and center-extending. I wonder if there is not something of that tension expressed in the petitions of our central prayer: "Thy kingdom come, thy will be done" seems to be the attractive center for which we yearn; "Give us today our daily bread" (or, as some read it, "our bread for *tomorrow*") seems to acknowledge the strength for mission we require to express and extend that kingdom and reign. "Center-extending" is another way of beginning to describe mission and the impact that total ministry has in that context.

Mission has always been the vocation for the church. We are not suggesting any new tangent here, nor is this focus apart from what we acknowledge as our tradition. What we now call total ministry is really recalling what ministry was/is meant to be. Total ministry once again tries to recast "ministry" in terms of individual people related in community: to recapture that sense of organism that tends to get swallowed up in "organization," in "institution," and in the old systems for keeping things in place.

We do seem to fight to preserve the old systems within which we function with some degree of comfort, sometimes with little regard to the effectiveness of those systems. The sense of "tradition" as "the faith once delivered to the saints" has an odd ring to it when placed alongside gospel passages saying that foxes may have holes, and birds may have nests but Jesus' followers may not be so materially and systemically secure (Luke 9:58; Matt. 8:20). In the context of what discipleship entails, those passages suggest a vocation to *trust* that God will be in the midst of things and things yet to come even if it may not be in terms of the system(s) we espouse and endorse; God may yet be revealing will and purpose that the "saints" have failed to recognize. Conversely, we also trust that God may use the systems to which we are accustomed, perhaps to challenge the custom attached to the system or to move it more gracefully into God's orbit and out of our control, beyond our preoccupations. In any case, we need to be far more discerning about the differences between a living tradition and ecclesiastical or cultic custom and remain open to the One who calls.

Vocation Beyond System

A Vocation to Partnership

All baptized Christians have a vocation, outlined and given direction in the baptismal covenant. That covenant is a communal affirmation to which individuals subscribe; by doing so they become part of the community's ministry. As another way of expressing the total ministry of the community and the individual's ministry in it, I have suggested an alternative to traditional letters of transfer, which no longer seem to serve the church as well as they might have been intended to. For many years in quite a few denominations, such letters have gone with people when they moved from one place to another and/or from one congregation to another. It seems appropriate that, with or without such a letter, a person entering a congregation as a new member be asked to prepare to reaffirm baptismal vows at the time of the bishop's visitation, or on some other occasion when membership is recognized and affirmed, making a public statement that "I am part of this community's covenant ministry" and receiving the parish community's declaration of support in its common life in Christ.[1] In the Episcopal Church tradition, the bishop is the symbol of the church's unity; the bishop's visit is a good time for local commitment to be expressed in a wider context. I have also been present at a United Methodist church's incorporation of new members. There I was aware of this same sense of membership as partnership in mission and service.

To be sure, this active, potential alternative to paper work (letters of transfer) does a number on those statistics that measure numbers and geographical distributions, but is that the best system for affirming and assisting ministry? Or is it expressive of some other need to diagnose— as preface to joy or grief about—the system? (Consider this line of thinking: *Now that we know what's wrong or weak or needful, we can do something about it.* This may have more to do with old systems of control than we have realized. Once we know what's wrong, we can fix it with ways to get people in, keep some out, develop new programs and strategies, and even write new books!)

The reaffirmation of baptismal vows is a focused way of remembering our identity as a covenant people. As people subscribe to the covenant, they become part of the community's ministry as individuals yet as inseparable members of the community. Here 1 Corinthians 12 is especially helpful. Paul's focus is on the *coordination* of gifts by the Spirit, rather than on the individual merits of each gift. Contemporary "sensitivity" has changed that focus to warm the hearts and activate some motions of the gifted, but this tack devalues the sense of what Paul is saying.

I remember a well-attended "gifts workshop" some years ago in a parish. The central activity for the day was an exercise where each person walked around with a piece of blank paper on his or her back. Others were instructed to write down on those sheets of paper the "gifts" they believed that particular person to possess. It was a fun exercise, and people were genuinely surprised by the insights of others, and everyone went home feeling good late that afternoon. It was several weeks before we realized that we had no idea where to go from there, because the gifts, celebrated only as individual, were not linked or coordinated. It was a time of affirmation without a sense of direction. While some had a sense of "what I can do" in the parish, there was little sense of direction in and as community.

In 1 Corinthians 12, Paul keeps the proper priority on the giver and coordinator of gifts. That sense of priority provides, as Paul suggests, an equality of gifts, because these sometimes strange and diverse gifts really work only as they are bound or "glued" together by the Spirit.

So one's vocation is not to a categorical system or to an old set of customs that may be recognized as systems. It may take many forms and result in many "ministries." But in fact there is one ministry of the one body, which is Christ's ministry as exercised through that body. All vocations contribute to the efficacy of that one ministry, expressed in mission. And here is where we run into a confusion of "centers"; for the terms *my ministry, my priesthood, my episcopate, my pastorate,* long-favored parts of our ecclesiastical job descriptions, really deny God's centrality to ministry and the impetus of God's Spirit in empowering and coordinating the mission of Christ's body. It is always Christ's ministry and not "mine." I am coordinated (co-ordained in baptism) to orbit with others around the center who is God, and in that community we are attracted to God and sent by God.

It is important from time to time to take vocation out of its institutional context, where it plays into some old systems of call and worthiness. Some vocations become set apart as "better" or "holier" than others, or "higher up the ladder" or more important. It helps to refocus or, better, to *remember* the meaning of *church* as "called out together" (ecclesia). We might want to explore that meaning of *church*, and perhaps we would arrive at a sense of "being called out" as "to reenter in a different way."

We might feel called to think in terms of being called out of a set of systems that we identify as either "churchly" or "worldly" models in order to be converted to another way of doing life—what Jesus expressed as the kingdom of God. "The time is fulfilled, and the kingdom of God has come near; repent, and believe in the good news" (Mark 1:15). It is as if Jesus is saying, *Look, the systems you have been using have not worked too well for you, and so God is setting a new adventure before you—where you are out of control and God does reign; that's going to mean some changes, but, you have to believe me, it is good news!* Our vocation in baptism is to accept the ministry in which we reenter the world, born again of water and the Spirit, with the vision of its transformation and redemption as God's world. We learn and promise to witness to the Way that leads to the recognition of God's ownership of the society, the culture, or the "world" in which we minister.

That perspective also does something to our understanding of what holiness is. Instead of making holiness peculiar or special or even ordained, we are given the vision to discover holiness welling up in what we call "ordinary," even in the ministry expressed by every baptized person in the community of faith. That is an adventure, full of holy surprises, again conducive to holy fear. One of the great surprises may be that God has beat us—gone before us—into the world and has been at work there for some time, perhaps even in ways we fail to appreciate and don't accept. It is amazing how the spirit of the "sabbath controversies" that marked Jesus' ministry is still alive today. The contemporary version of church versus world provides continuing testimony to the power that categorical systems have in reaction to ministry that moves beyond them. Our enslavement to systems becomes embarrassingly apparent when we find ways to take the acceptance and forgiveness we know in Christ and codify them as means for excluding others from shared ministry.

Too Much "Model" as Ministry

At another pole (and I am afraid there are more than two), there is an apparent need to force *total ministry* into the vocabulary of every baptized person. This takes shape most often in attempts to describe every daily action as "ministry"—which is in itself one of the church's "ministries" of presumption. It is as if we are presuming to say, "What you are doing will mean much more once we put our labels on it," as if that raises daily work and witness to a higher and better level.

I remember what happened in one parish that had lost its rector and was entering upon its own exploration of how total ministry could help them articulate ministry. At first they were encouraged by a regional vicar (on bishop's staff) to form various functional groups, including committees such as a worship committee, grounds and building committee, and so on. One such group was formed and called the pastoral care committee. When I stopped by for an informal visit, the members of that committee admitted to a paralysis; "pastoral care" was what the priest did, especially in counseling. Because they felt untrained and inadequate, they were doing nothing at all, except to worry about their inability to function. Of course the congregation had been taking care of its members for years—bringing food at times of illness or grief, giving rides to doctors' appointments, calling up to sympathize, to listen, to share good news, visiting in the hospital, hearing "confessions" and offering timely absolutions and/or counsel, and so on and on. That is pastoral care, but the label didn't help. It wasn't needed. The internal support ministry of the parish was in fine shape. They simply needed to be looking outward from that strength. They did not need to rearticulate and birth a new but old model. They needed to let it die, so that the ministry could live.

The Baptismal Vocation

Vocation is the response to inspiration, not to a system. It leads us to promise to be part of a God-centered company that lives in grace—in the relationship we have with God through Jesus Christ. What is grace? It is God including us in the flow of life orbiting around the center, which is God. Vocation is then our acceptance of the Spirit's coordination of our gifts, and the Spirit provides the energy, the momentum, and the context to live out the promise and to extend the center in whatever arenas may be offered—whether that be workplace, home, school, or play environments. There is no recognizable limit to viable vocational expression so long as we remember that vocation is a community enterprise, and that the life of the community is fed far better with imagination in expressing tradition, rather than by custom alone.

To "have a vocation" is to be baptized. To "go into the ministry" is to be baptized. Throughout much of its history, the church has denied that vocational scope and given higher credence and respect to clergy vocations. The church's emerging tradition is being guided back to an awareness of the breadth of vocation to ministry, notably in terms of its expression by the laity. But as an essential part of an understanding of total ministry, the church must *listen* to those who are ministering as Christ's body. Listening is more important than devising systems to "empower" the laity, those who are already expressing the Spirit's power. I see this whole notion of "empowering the laity" as being condescending to those who have been unable to do anything all along, which is far from the case. That same mindset has also retranslated the word *lay* to divert its roots in *laos* to a secondary and more popular sense of "inexpert."

I need to confess that the critical view I have just put forth has not considered well enough some of the fine work being done in harnessing and channeling the ministry expressed by the laity. In print and in person there are some fine witnesses to how well a turned-on laity can function when challenged by suitable programs that first listen to them: the spiritual hungers they feel and the competence they have in meeting those needs and hungers in others beyond the church walls. A newer sense of empowerment has been emerging that acknowledges the power of the laity and seeks to respect and include that in the ministry of the coordinated body of Christ.

Some of the difficulty I experience in this area, however, has to do with that whole sense of program. The best work is being done in mid-sized to larger parishes where there are financial and personnel resources not always available in the smaller church. As a result, it is often difficult to translate good programs into a setting where such resources are very limited, in terms of numbers—dollars and people. That is a programmatic reality we are still learning to address.

The situation is different in the small church, usually due to the absence of full-time clergy. So many people remember when "Reverend So-and-So came and did it for us, and he was so kind and such a character. Ah, those were the days." Many small congregations are still mourning the loss of a ministry model that is no longer appropriate. They lose their sense of baptismal vocation in recurring waves of nostalgia. Being introduced to well-conceived programs that seem unachievable for their size becomes occasion for loss of confidence because the programs remind them of the old model they miss. While it is difficult to document this nostalgic mood statistically, it is part of the pulse of a place: the deeply rooted reluctances, humilities, strengths, and memories that are so much of a congregation's personality.

The legacy of the old system with a seminary-trained ordained person in or available to every parish most of the time was that "the minister" did the telling of the story. The minister—the pastor—knew the Bible. The minister was good at counseling. Few parishioners could claim those gifts without being deemed presumptuous; so "ministry" and "laity" were almost contradictory terms, separated by Religious Knowledge.

In the small church, especially in remote areas, the issue is not to release the laity's ministry but to inspire confidence in telling the story and living it out intentionally. Ministry is happening under any number of designations, including "neighborliness." Church membership and living in the small community cannot be separated.

Again, I return to the very questionable assumption that there is a radical difference between ordained ministry and unordained ministry. There is one ministry. Why do we need to designate some of it "lay"?

Truth

Perhaps it would be helpful to reexamine our focus on "truth" and what that is as part of our tradition and our continuing life together. I was privileged to study with Kenneth Woollcombe during my three years at the General Theological Seminary in New York City. He had the wonderful capacity to encourage and demonstrate theological *thinking* as the need to go beyond just getting the facts straight; in that process he could sometimes set a class on its ear by challenging assumptions we had accepted.

On one such occasion, he took on the prayer of Saint John Chrysostom that helps to conclude the morning and evening prayer offices in *The Book of Common Prayer*. He said in effect that the good saint had it all backwards in his petition that we be granted "in this world knowledge of your truth, and in the age to come life everlasting." We already have life everlasting, Woollcombe said. That is the central truth of the Cross and the Resurrection. Truth grows in that sense of having everlasting life until, as Paul hopes, "I will know fully, even as I have been fully known" (1 Cor. 13:12).

A sound theological presentation loses something in a student's translation some thirty years later, nor was Woollcombe's point that truth is unavailable to us. But again, it is something of a question about priorities. John's gospel is particularly helpful to me in understanding where truth resides; John expresses it in terms of relationship: "I am the way, and the truth, and the life." "I am . . . the truth" (John 14:6). To know the truth is first of all to know Jesus Christ, and that truth sets us free from other priorities and becomes the first fact of our life. In that relationship we continue to grow in the truth of what the life in Christ entails and how we express it in our daily conduct: the kind of thing Paul seems to have in mind as he urges the Philippians to "live your life in a manner worthy of the gospel of Christ" (Phil. 1:27).

Simply put, the priority of the ministering community is to maintain and grow in its relationship with the living Lord in a spirit consistent with Jesus' assertion in John 5:17, "My Father is still working, and I also am working," or in the livelier translation offered in *The New English Bible*, "My Father has never yet ceased his work, and I am working, too." It is not a priority of that community to develop categorical systems that become the focus of worth-ship, partnered with litmus tests for truth. The community needs ways to order its common life, but those ways are a means to express the group's central relationship; they are not an end—a codified system used as the criterion for judgment in preference to a more central reliance on the throne of mercy around which we all orbit.

Working at a diocesan camp in Minnesota one summer, I was talking with the young waterfront director. She had recently transferred into a Bible college somewhere in the Midwest and was lamenting the fact that she found so little room for growth there. Everything was set and truth was well ordered. "It's just a new bondage," was her pained assessment. Questions were not encouraged. The truth was set in place, and she did not feel it set her free.

The relationship with Christ opens doors and windows, and leads us beyond still waters into new territories and visions. The model-systems of which we become overfond often stop the journey and wall in the household; they can become a "new bondage" when we worship them. Do we throw everything out? No. Is it chaos? (Sometimes it feels that way, but even then we remember that chaos was the context for Creation.) No. It is trust that our Father has never yet ceased his work, and that Jesus Christ is working, too, in the power of the Holy Spirit. That is the fundamental spirit of total ministry, which acknowledges that the ministering community is attracted to its Lord and sent by the same Lord to be attractive to others in his name. To go out selling categorical systems and models as truth is safer than the dangerous living that often characterizes mission. But selling systems is not the church's true vocation. Instead, our vocation has something to do with the systemic revolution explicit in the invitation to repent, and believe in the Good News.

CHAPTER 2

Who's the Highest?

Total ministry has become a fairly widespread term, with task forces, individual judicatories, and various other groups exploring this area; they arrive at their own definitions which can be quite diverse. These are healthy contributions to the rich texture of ministry in Christ's body—until they become models or systems for others to adopt as "the right way."

Whatever direction these various attempts take, a practical difficulty still emerges in the preoccupation with ordination and subordination (as in licensing for various in-house duties). In the Episcopal Church, various licenses are prescribed for laypeople to perform certain duties involving worship and pastoral functions. Lay readers, who may lead public worship, and lay eucharistic ministers (LEMs), who may bring the Sacrament of the altar to shut-ins unable to attend corporate worship, are the two licenses most used in our diocese. The licensing process, and the subtle ways it is linked to looking like clergy or doing clergy things, begins to move into a hierarchical model we are trying to overcome.

In this context I remember a Palm Sunday many years ago. We had come directly home from church, and my wife and I were in the kitchen, preparing lunch. Our kindergarten son came in from outside. He stood in the door and announced, "I can tell you what the people said when Jesus rode into town on a donkey." He paused to collect his thoughts. "Hosanna, I'm the highest."

There does seem to be some concern about who's the highest as people enter into total-ministry exploration. Outsiders frequently ask us in the Diocese of Nevada about our calling and ordination process for local clergy; how or when or if those called locally vote in diocesan convention; and how do those locally called relate to the so-called "professional" clergy, meaning those who were educated on the seminary track. In many of the inquiries there is a hint of nervousness about what "they" (local clergy) will do to change "our" (professionally trained) systems of being in–charge professionals. So there is at least a slight flavor of politics in what for generations has been a clergy-controlled church. "Who's the highest" has a great deal to do with control.

While we do have responses to those questions, we acknowledge our own discomfort that the church is still operating on a clergy-centered system, even though they are allowing qualified laypeople to assume some of the duties traditionally reserved for clergy and on occasion to vest like clergy while doing them. Total ministry is the ministry of *all* the baptized, the greatest percentage of whom are laity. It is not my intent to be congregational or anticlerical. I do have difficulty with some of the "calls" to ordained ministry that happen apart from a community context and stay out of that context until an ordination process begins.

Calls to Ministry

One young woman came to see me somewhat nervously with a "call" to "go to seminary." As we talked about how she experienced that call, we discovered an urgency in her to know more about God's interaction with this creation and humanity and to feel a more intimate part of that. She had shared that sense of call and of need with no one else. I asked her to go back to her parish community and form a small group of people who might explore her sense of direction with her; I also asked that she include not only close friends, but also some acquaintances. Two or three months later she returned, a happier and more self-assured woman. In the mini-community she had formed, she had discovered a need for knowledge that could be met in other ways than through attendance at a seminary. Her group also helped her to work out other priorities on her journey, including financial management. So there was indeed a call, but it took shape and found direction in the community. Self-selection for ordination, or individual response alone, needs a community context. That is another way of expressing the coordinated gifts described in 1 Corinthians 12 (see chapter 1).

Self-selection also produces other interesting "calls." The ones that I am most careful about seem to come out of anger, though they are rarely articulated in those terms. I remember one very talented young man who knew he was called to the priesthood; he had even had a recurring dream that verified the call. As we met together over a period of weeks and as we explored the dream's content and his response, it appeared that the dream might actually have been pointing him *away from* ordination; in his anger he was really out to "fix the church" according to his own prescription. It happened that, as he continued to act out his anger in various ways, he was finally confronted by his parish community. At that point he moved to a more "biblical" and controlling religious expression.

Not all instances of self-selection for ordination are misleading. People do hear strong calls to serve in ordained roles. One mature woman came to see me with such a sense of call. We spent four or five months, meeting once a month, to explore her spiritual journey and to reflect on the responses of her own very affirming community. Her progress through seminary and now as a priest has been strongly rooted in community, and she exhibits a clear gift listening to and hearing the community of which she is a part.

I can cite my own "ministry development" as another case in point. A very dramatic call to ordained ministry led me to consult with a local rector, after some period of resistance. In turn, and without discussion with anyone else, I was sent to the bishop's office, where I was interviewed and told which seminary I wanted to attend. An appointment with the standing committee followed in due time, and the committee was especially interested in which Zabriskies I owned as relatives. In all fairness, the bishop then allowed me to take two years off before seminary, during which I began to learn something about the mystery of Christian community from a chaplain at a church preparatory school where I taught. With at least a minimal and somewhat idealized understanding of community, I entered seminary and there was thrust into the struggle for community in a group of young to not-so-young men in the early 1960s. It took the laity and some very special clergy in subsequent parishes to teach me the ways in which community functions and how I fit into that and serve in that context.

One of my most cherished memories is of a senior warden who called me up after I had been the church's rector for several months. After some pleasant conversation, he gently reminded me, "You know, Stewart, you don't have to do it all by next Tuesday. We can help, too."

And help they did, as we moved more and more into community ministry instead of priestly "dedication" and control. "By next Tuesday" has become a byword I now use to remind me of my place in community and my reliance on those relationships.

I know solitary calls happen, but I believe they must always be tested in the local community before they go on to any next "step" in an ordination process. For it is one of the ministering community's tasks of discernment to discover who among them is needed to serve in a variety of capacities necessary to the work of the whole body in that place. That is, if you will, one of the so-called ministries of the laity.

Who's Worthy?

A traditional problem surfaces when vocations are discerned within the community. Our descriptive vocabulary tells it all. So-and-so is *raised up* for the priesthood or for the diaconate. Such people are ready to move higher on the ecclesiastical ladder, somehow set apart as different from their brother and sister ministers in the same community. Then they are *sent away* to be formed, to gather adequate knowledge, and to learn the craft of their holy orders. The next step is to *seek employment,* usually in some community other than the one from which they emerged and one that has had no part in their formation. While that has had some advantages for the church over the years, it does raise some other questions as well.

The Question of "Holy Orders"

The first question has to do with the designation of clergy as in "holy orders." According to *The Book of Common Prayer,* there are four orders of ministry: laity, bishops, priests, and deacons. Are only three of them holy? This is the kind of ecclesi-talk that creates systems we might want to question. In the process of setting eligibilities for entering and completing the ordination process, a great deal of energy is placed upon *worthiness,* though we may be reluctant to call it that. There are frequent attempts to create boundaries around whom God or a ministering community may call into "holy orders," and in doing that we communicate that these holy orders are more important than the rest of the church's leadership and function. No one will deny the importance of holy character in the administration of the Sacraments and, indeed, in all Christian conduct.

But it might put ministry in a clearer focus to rescind entirely what many see as "worthiness" canons or resolutions. In the Episcopal Church, canons are the necessary structure for the denomination's organization, and some canons are devoted to eligibility and process for ordination. Resolutions are statements of intent, designed to put forth some point of view with regard to any number of different issues, including eligibility for ordination. An initiative to put "worthiness" canons and resolutions behind us might refocus that particular vocational process to allow for (1) God's initiative and (2) the local community's integrity as the context for vocational discernment. The process still moves beyond a solely congregational context, as people in the ordination process also must meet with people on a commission on ministry and a standing committee, with representation from the wider diocesan or judicatory community; those representatives also explore both the person's sense of call and the person's relationship to the local congregation.

The Question of Knowledge

The second question raised by the corporate discernment of vocation has to do with knowledge and who has it. For many centuries in the church's life, the clergy were the educated class. Even into my own generation, it has been assumed that clergy are sent away to seminary to learn what the rest of you really don't know much about; and many of us set about our ordained experience by sharing all that knowledge with those entrusted to our care whether they needed it or not!

I remember my first year as a curate in a New York City parish. Three young adults came requesting baptism, and the parish rector assigned me the task of their preparation, ostensibly because they were young and I was young. What a great store of knowledge I shared with them over the next few months, more to my own satisfaction than to their edification, though I could not realize that then. It was a testimony to their endurance that they did come to the baptismal font one Sunday after the main service. There something wonderful happened that had little to do with my instruction. After the baptisms, everyone hung around, holding hands, even hugging here and there. Now, this was in the days when Episcopalians rarely touched one another, but those present were acting out the reality of the community into which they had been initiated—and taught one young curate what it was really all about.

Nowadays, thanks to efforts such as Education for Ministry (EFM), a "portable" course for lay theological education and reflection developed at the School of Theology of the University of the South in Sewanee, Tennessee; KERYGMA, an extended course in Bible study; and other biblical/historical theological education materials, we have a proportionately articulate and increasingly well-trained laity, many of whom have a sense of theological perspective and context that seminary education does not always provide.

Education is really the task of the whole community, and its priorities are threefold for the ministering and missionary community: (1) to know the story, the biblical witness; (2) to know what the story means, the theology that gives the story momentum and the history that details its context and impact; and (3) to know how to live the story, in terms of liturgy, history and future, evangelism and mission, *as part of the Spirit-coordinated community.*

In the context of total ministry, then, we do not need to ordain others who will know more than the rest of us. We do need to ordain some among us to help the body of Christ remain centered spiritually; in the Episcopal Church that is expressed through regular participation in the Sacraments, which assure us of the divine presence in the midst of our life together. Other denominations find other ways of recalling the same presence. So we call some to be priests, to gather the community for sacramental worship; we call others to be deacons, to bring before the body the opportunities for mission and to encourage the means for training for and responding to those opportunities. Other denominations have different ways and titles for doing much the same thing, still the same Spirit is at work coordinating the body of Christ.

Local Calls and Theological Education

The Diocese of Nevada does ordain people who have been to seminary as well as those who are locally called. Seminary-trained clergy conform to all of the requirements of the appropriate canons and take the General Ordination Exams before they are considered for placement in a parish that can afford to pay them. Under the provisions of the Episcopal Church canon mentioned earlier (Canon III.9), parishes may also call "local clergy," who are trained in the diocese to serve only in the parish that calls them. They are not paid, and many work at full-time jobs outside the church.

In the Diocese of Nevada, the process of calling people to ordination as local clergy is a relatively simple one. It resides particularly in a sense of the Spirit-centeredness of total ministry considered above. The decision to enter into the calling process may arise out of a variety of circumstances, many of them economic: lack of sufficient income to pay a full-time priest's stipend and benefits; the decision to stop devoting the greatest percentage of the parish budget to clergy support and look toward a newer expression of mission; too few people in a remote parish.

When it appears that a local congregation is ready to begin a process of call, several things may happen. First, it notifies the bishop of its intent, usually through the regional vicar; the bishop notifies the diocesan commission on ministry that Saint Somebody's is beginning the process it hopes will result in a call or commendation for a member to become a local priest and/or deacon. Then the congregation may undertake a gifts discovery workshop under the direction of a diocesan staff member or someone else trained to assist congregations in that way. This may occur over a period of weeks or months, or it may be a two-day weekend event. The content and intent of that workshop is to explore the gifts available to the parish and the ways in which those gifts are coordinated for the ministry of the whole parish, everyone in it.

In the next step, the congregation undertakes a study of the offices (priest and/or deacon) to which it will call. With that goes the instruction that this is a *listening and calling* process and not an election. No names are put forth at any time prior to the commendation itself. It is meant to be understood from the beginning that the Spirit directs the call(s). Together with and subsequent to the study is a time of prayer. One month before a scheduled commendation or call, the bishop calls the diocese to prayer for the "calling" congregation(s); the congregation itself is asked to pray for the Spirit's guidance as it prepares for a call. If at any time it appears that political expertise or electioneering has taken over the process, it is terminated. It is interesting to note, too, that on occasions when such electioneering is not detected, it still shows up and the commendation does not result in a call. That has happened only twice in my experience. It is more than interesting how quickly the reliance on a different spirit can be detected in the commendation forms I receive. In one such instance, where the parish was trying to call a local deacon, a number of the commendation forms put forth one name; in every case each contained a little note about the rector's failings and the existing deacon's inattentions. A different spirit, indeed!

I need to note here that self-selection is not a sin! People do hear calls to ordination that they then bring before the community. That begins the process of preparing for and attending seminary. In the process of calls for local clergy, self-selection can be a distraction from a process that relies most heavily on prayer as the instrument of discernment. Knowing "who wants it" tends to avoid the surprises offered by the Spirit.

The commendation itself happens at a specific time, always in the context of a Sunday Eucharist. Parish members are given a commendation form, which includes several prayers for guidance and space at the bottom to fill in the name(s) of people for a given office. (Some parishes use this same process for the calling of lay eucharistic ministers.) The forms are placed on the altar as a part of the offertory. Following the service, they are gathered up and sent, without perusal, to the bishop. The bishop ascertains that a responsible percentage of the congregation has participated and then proceeds to determine whether a call has happened. In the event that someone(s) has been so called, the bishop phones her/him/them and asks that they give this call prayer and reflection for a period of time. In the case of a parish calling a deacon where there is a rector, the rector may also be notified. In parishes served by a regional vicar, the person(s) so called may be encouraged to talk with the vicar also. Otherwise, no public announcement is made until the person called has accepted the call.

The announcement is made to the congregation that, in turn, affirms the call. This affirmation may take many forms, though usually it is done with some acclamation by voice when the call is announced to the parish, perhaps in response to the question, "Will you uphold and walk with this person (these people) in the call they have accepted?"

What follows has been called a number of things, none of which is particularly descriptive, but it is a time for exploring the *shared* nature of the journey that continues. Members of the diocesan commission on ministry visit the parish at a prearranged time to listen with the congregation to the story of the person(s) called. It is a time for sharing spiritual journey: the road traveled so far as well as the road that stretches out ahead *for the whole congregation.* This visit includes a reminder that the person(s) called will not be allowed to study and prepare alone; if that happens, the process stops. The congregation, or a good number from it, will study with those called. Again, those called have not been called to know more than the rest of the parish. Christian education, *theological education,* is a part of everyone's vocation.

How that education progresses depends on many variables. While we have definite canonical requirements for study, it is also true that people called to orders are rarely Christian beginners. Some have been studying for years; others have been active participants in the Diocesan School for Theology, together with other members from the same congregation. That school for theology meets twice a year for one evening each week for six consecutive weeks. Required biblical, theological, and historical courses are offered over a period of three years, with additional courses for those who have moved beyond the requirements. The school serves not only people in the local ordination process, but also (and mostly) others who see Christian education as an ongoing responsibility. Those in the ordination process do further work with a regional vicar, who suggests further reading and reflects on that with them.

The material offered in these urban gatherings also travels to more rural areas as weekend or monthly offerings. It offers basic courses as well as more advanced material. The educational program does not start from ground zero, but it assures that the people called and their congregations "cover the bases" together as is appropriate for them.

It is not required that a full seminary-type course be accomplished before ordination as local deacon or priest. Indeed, such a requirement would give some justification to the fear that local clergy are "second-class" clergy, which is far from our experience of those so ordained. People are called to orders by their congregations out of need for that function within the body. To extend the period of preparation over too many years risks the danger of disappointment and even depression in a parish. Such feelings can dissipate the energy required for study and the missionary life of the congregation that continues during this process. It is important to note that the life and witness of the parish *does* continue during this period of study and congregational reformation. Sharing in the preparation of one or two of its members for orders is a *part* of the congregation's ongoing life. Actually, it is a preface to the kind of continuing Christian education that could mark and enhance the life of every ministering community.

To that end, the candidates for orders under Canon III.9 sign an agreement with the bishop that includes the commitment to lifelong continuing education.[1] (Continuing education needs to be a given no matter what ordination track one takes.) While it has not yet been made explicit, the intent remains that the congregation will continue to participate in the life of learning as a part of its shared vocation.

As the process toward local ordination progresses, examinations happen as requirements are met, but here again we rely on a special context. After a written, objective scripture exercise that assures some biblical literacy (knowing the story), the examinations are done in community. It seems contrary to our understanding of total ministry to send a candidate out of the room with a blue book to produce in a matter of several hours what he or she knows. Instead we ask the candidates to make several short presentations on specific questions provided by the diocesan commission on ministry. Presentations are made in the context of the candidates' own communities with commission members present. Different occasions are set aside for presentations on scripture, the faith of the church, and liturgy. The parish community is invited to respond, to question, to discuss; and in that dynamic we get a sense of how the community expresses its internal relationships and its missionary purpose and where the prospective ordinand fits in to that. To date we have had some wonderful experiences in scriptural and theological discussion and a growing sense of the work of all the people in liturgy.

We also made some mistakes. On one occasion we tried to combine two candidates and two congregations for the examinations. Even though the two parishes shared the same region, their dynamics did not mix in such a way as to provide stimulating discussion. This left the candidates in an awkward position. They were not sure who should answer when, or who should ask what. Later reflecting on the exam, the diocesan commission on ministry saw that we were beginning to do a "model" and have a "system," in an attempt to coordinate for our own benefit what the Spirit was not coordinating. It did not work.

Underlying this whole process, then, is our understanding of the

Spirit as the one who coordinates the church body for ministry. It is in the Spirit that we call from among us people to be priest and deacon; it is the same Spirit who coordinates, who binds the congregation and the diocese together as a well-centered community called for worship and to missionary service.

Who Are These . . . ?

We need to put some names and faces on the local-ordination process, lest it seem only a theoretical exercise. A complete catalog of our Canon 9 "local clergy" need not be offered here, but a sampling does help to understand both the texture of the total-ministry process as well as the Spirit's wisdom in call.

Dale had been the pharmacist in his community for many years when he was called to study for priesthood with his congregation. In the local drug store, near the town's junior and senior high schools and complete with soda fountain, Dale had been a community gatherer in a very real sense. And so he has continued to be since his ordination as priest, gathering the community for sacramental worship and the sharing of the Word.

Madge and Estelle had been long-time residents of their community when they were both commended for priesthood. Madge ran the local hardware-plus-a-lot-of-other-goods store, where people gathered not only to buy, but also to chat and share bits of their lives with one another. Estelle was equally active in the small community, a former mining town on the side of a mountain. Both women were known for their unpretentious but strong faith.

Bonnie was already active in jail ministry when she was commended for the diaconate. She had noticed a void in that ministry, due to some abuses by a former chaplain. As she found a way in to the jail administration's trust, the ministry among the inmates was revived. To this day, that ministry continues, but not by Bonnie alone. She has taken others with her. Together with laity in her own congregation and beyond, Bonnie has also been instrumental in the development of a food outreach center, open five days a week and staffed by lay volunteers; a shelter for homeless women and children that has become a thriving ecumenical ministry; a single-residence-occupancy program for homeless people and families working to reenter the mainstream, which also has broad ecumenical support. Bonnie honors the charge in the ordination service for deacons to "interpret to the church the needs, concerns, and hopes of the world" *and* to activate the church's response by training and helping people to move out into those same needs, concerns, and hopes. She does not work alone.

Carolyn, Lionel, and Jim all serve as deacons in one small parish. One works with handicapped children, another in health services to people with HIV/AIDS, and the other as a corrections officer. That's what they call "work." In addition, they work to stimulate the parish's commitment to reach out to the hungry by stocking a parish pantry for distribution; they hold up particular ministries among at-risk youth; and they continue to encourage visions of where the church can offer specific service in its urban community. It is a slow process, but they are persistent people.

Burt is a pediatrician, commended by his parish for priesthood in the early days of Nevada's total-ministry development. A gifted musician and teacher, he helps his own congregation as well as other congregations understand the rhythm and momentum of liturgy, where worship leads to service. As a physician concerned with health, he brings that focus to the gathered parish. With excellent lay leadership, the congregation has undertaken a process of ministry development that is generating considerable energy—and health!

Ken, a local priest, works as a respiratory technician in a rural hospital and also runs a mail route through remote central Nevada. He was called by the diocesan commission on ministry from a parish that was not ready to go through the commendation process on its own. There were too few members and too many of those old memories that can create an interesting family system in a congregation; in that context it was difficult to accommodate the calling process, and yet the area stood in great need for a local priest. Ken's gifts for bringing people together had already been tested in the community. His care for people in the hospital was well known and went beyond his professional responsibilities. He was an effective leader in a local service organization. And he was well known in town and out on the range. The local parish applauded and affirmed his call. At his ordination to the priesthood, a group of people on the mail route came in and provided a celebratory barbecue; members of other denominations joined in the worship; and even some old members, lapsed for perhaps forgotten reasons, turned up. Since that time, the parish has been growing in spite of local economic problems. Communities way out of town have been asking for some local worship, and the parish has called two people to serve as deacon and priest. For Ken has learned not to do it all. He gathers the people for the strength and renewal of the Sacrament and, in the absence of a deacon, sends them out in the power of the Spirit. Then he goes out on a mail route and begins to gather others for worship in community. Ken has been introducing me to places in Nevada I never knew were there.

Kay works for the National Park Service and was called by her congregation to priesthood. Her study process was crowded with parish members, who continue to study with her and on their own. Having already called an energetic and highly effective deacon in Shirley, the parish has a lively ministry providing local respite care. As priest Kay gathers the community in a holy sense of being a part of God's creation, responsible in that creation as stewards of it. Her particular gift is to see the sacramental nature of all life, and that is received as an important dimension of the parish's life and witness. The parish also knows that she cannot do it all alone; her professional and family responsibilities require considerable time. They have called a second person to prepare for priesthood.

It is difficult to stay with the promise not to catalog the entire list of local clergy. When the commendation process is followed carefully and the Spirit is given the control, the result is the call of wise and holy people who reflect well the spirit of the calling congregation. It is a strong temptation to celebrate all of them here. But these few names and details give some sense of the variety and texture of the total-ministry process as it relates to local ordination.

But we need to repeat again and again that the local ordination process does not stand alone. It arises out of the ministry of the whole congregation as that group offers its life for the guidance of the Holy Spirit. The resultant calls to orders do not excuse anyone in the parish from ministry; those calls simply seek to endow and provide for the sacramental center that energizes the ministry of the congregation in its community and beyond.

Roles: Priesthood, Diaconate, and Congregation

In writing about ordained roles in the church I necessarily refer to the
traditional threefold ordained ministry of the Episcopal Church: bishop,
priest, and deacon. I do believe, however, that even when the titles
change or when some of the theology is expressed differently by other
denominations, some of the core issues remain as we try to understand
the roles and the limits of ordained people.

The Role of Priest

In the Diocese of Nevada we tend to oversimplify the roles of ordained
ministry to some degree, for the sake of a basic clarity. We say that the
priest is the community gatherer, responsible for the sacramental worship
of the local community. The priest may have other gifts as well, but with
our locally called and trained clergy we are careful to assure that *every*
gift is not offered simultaneously. Real or imagined omnicompetence is
a method of control and does not allow a congregation to express its
shared ministry. We ask that the call to priesthood be supplemented by
an intentional offering of one other gift besides the ministry of the Sacraments. For some that may be as preacher, for which the candidate will
be trained and licensed. But not all priests are called to preaching (which
might also be said about some seminary-trained clergy). Some may be
gifted as hospital visitors or as school board members or for any number
of commitments in the community. We need also to remember that
many of our local clergy are employed in full-time jobs in their communities, and they are not paid for their exercise as priest or deacon in the
local parish.

    In the earlier days of the diocese's commitment to total ministry, the
old system of depending on a rector or priest-in-charge to "do it for us"
kept sneaking into the newly designed process. It was easy to confer the
honor of omnicompetence on those locally called, though that was far
from the intent of local commendation. In some instances we saw that,
once a person was called to prepare for orders, congregants viewed this
person differently, as if ordination were going to change the person. The
wish behind this? Once ordained, the new priest would be endowed with
the will and the ability to do for the congregation the ministry to which

the congregation was called. In one or two cases, we found the ordained person beginning to believe this scenario, and pastoral intervention and education was necessary.

Old systems die hard, and we cannot yet claim a total victory. It will take at least another generation for truly shared ministry to become the tradition, for systemic reordering to become a deeply rooted reality, though we are well on our way. Once congregations discover their own gifts for administering a parish and their resources for doing mission work in their own communities, they are unwilling to go back to "the old ways." They feel, quite rightly, that they would miss being-and-doing ministry.

The Need to Share Ministry

To honor the intent and the heart of total ministry, we ask every congregation to be clear about shared responsibilities. For some congregations that hardly goes beyond who is to clean the church, do the newsletter, set the altar, count the offering. For an increasing number of them, however, outreach into the community is a part of the parish ministry "package"; they have become more aware of (1) how much they have already been doing without calling it "ministry" in their daily rounds and common tasks and (2) how essential it is for a worshipping community to be servants beyond the altar and in the community where God has called them to be. A reprint from the introduction to *The Total Ministry Notebook (1990),* published by the Diocese of Nevada, helps us maintain this perspective and balance in the church's life as we continue to explore and grow in this ministering process:

> The Church
>   . . . is to offer itself in praise and thanksgiving through the Eucharist
>   . . . is to share the love of Jesus through its fellowship and mutual care
>   . . . is to continue in the Apostolic Faith and be strengthened in discipleship.
>   This is the life of the Church. Ministry is the instrument.

> The Church's mission is in and to the world to which he came
> and for which he died, and to live out what we know as
> Grace:
>> the relationship we have with God through Jesus Christ.

> The Church
>> . . . is to proclaim the Kingdom of God, the Good News of
>> God's free, total, unconditional love for everyone
>> . . . is to share with Christ in the ministry of reconciliation,
>> forgiveness, healing, and peace
>> . . . is to make a society in which all persons can love fully,
>> joyfully, peacefully, and justly.
>>> This is the mission of the Church. Ministry is the instrument.
>>> The Church needs the ministry of all its members to carry on
>> its life and to carry out its mission.2

The continuing challenge is to translate that perspective and balance into
practical embodied effect, where every congregation truly becomes in its
members a "letter of Christ" as ministers of the New Covenant (2 Cor.
3:1-3).

The Role of Deacon

If we can stretch the "letter of Christ" image just a bit, we can say that
deacons serve as postmasters, in bringing in the "mail" (needs, concerns,
hopes), sorting it out (helping to train some in the congregation for appropriate service and response), and sending it on (in dismissal for service). It is important to stress that the office of deacon is not primarily
a liturgical role. Whatever liturgical functions remain for the deacon
(reading the Gospel at the Eucharist, setting the table, and announcing
the dismissal) have integrity only as they express what the deacon is
doing *outside* the liturgical life of the congregation. It has been our experience that those called locally for diaconate are people who have been
exercising diaconal ministry in numbers of ways for some time, and we
have come to expect that prior activity in parish callings. Their commendation by and subsequent training with the congregation adds the dimension of communicator to the role they have already been carrying out.
As ordained deacons they are interpreting the "needs, hopes, and concerns

of the world" to the church, and they are learning to help marshal and
train parishioners who have good intentions for active ministry in the
community. Neither the deacon nor the priest is offered a solitary role.

I have said, and meant, that I cannot imagine being in a diocese without deacons, *real* deacons who understand and serve as models to all the
ministers (lay, priestly, episcopal) for the outlook of the church's mission. I also believe it is a mistake to ordain anyone a deacon who has not
shown in practice that she or he has a diaconal bearing in ministry. That
does keep the numbers realistic and honest. It is a question of "fit" rather
than of worthiness for the call to diaconate. There are many wonderful
people in our churches who do good things and whom we would like to
reward in some way. Ordination is not the appropriate way to do that. In
the case of calling deacons, the Spirit leads us to those who have the gift
of being able to challenge a perhaps reluctant parish community in con-
structive ways, because of what the potential deacons are doing already.

That leads to some surprise in the calling process. I have sometimes
presumed to think that I know in advance whom a parish will commend
for orders. It is more often true that the Spirit's vision is different from
my own, and that is a good reminder about who is really in charge of this
journey and this particular process.

Seminary-Trained Clergy

Our diocese does rely on the gifts of seminary-trained priests and deacons who are able to serve as trainers and educators, with an experience
of scholarship perhaps more intense than that of the local clergy. In
Nevada we are blessed by having full-time rectors of a few parishes, and
many of them understand their and our need for them to contribute from
their own training to the diocesan "journey." Regional vicars, clergy on
the bishop's staff who oversee from five to ten parishes, are all seminary
trained.

It is also our experience, however, that seminary-trained clergy usually need to be retrained for effective service in this diocese. The competi-
tive systems from which they may have come and the intense struggle
for community that is often part of seminary life do not prepare them for
the cooperative ministry and noncompetitive relationships between
clergy (no matter what their preparation track) and laity that we enjoy.

One seminary-trained priest explains that dynamic: "No one wants anyone else's job in this diocese!"

While accountability is a strong part of those relationships, control is not. Because of this we have recognized the need to retrain those from other diocesan systems whom we welcome into this diocese. We try to provide some structure for their call and their first year here. To that end our commission on ministry has developed a simple process that begins before a search is begun and continues through the first year of a new priest's service in the diocese. We will deal with that process in a subsequent chapter.3

In the search for full-time paid clergy, it is all too easy to lay the difficulty of securing suitable candidates at the feet of the seminaries, though to some extent our seminaries are responsible for recruitment problems. Yet seminaries are still meeting the expectations of a majority of the church, which looks back to the old systems that seemed to serve us so well for so many years. Much of the church is only beginning to acknowledge that there may be other ways to express parish-community ministry. There is the sometimes-defensive, partially accurate observation that the impetus toward the development of total ministry is economic, to provide ordained people in parishes that cannot afford full-time, seminary-trained clergy. If we are focused only on ordained people, there is some truth in that. But the greater truth is that the ministry of all the baptized is released from traditional clergy control into a whole new freedom, even when the initial reasons may be economic. So the sacrament of money, sometimes in its unavailability, can become the means to spiritual gifts.

Some seminaries are offering some training based on *listening* to what is beginning to happen in the church beyond seminary boundaries. It is a process different from sending seminarians out to do field work or on internships; it is one that sees the seminary's need to learn and respond to what the Spirit is saying to the churches. The work of John Kater, professor of ministry development at the Church Divinity School of the Pacific (CDSP) in Berkeley, California, and an imaginative refocusing on ministry concerns at Seabury-Western are significant steps, especially because they are receiving support in the larger seminary context. In CDSP's California context, with which I am the most familiar, support is significant in terms of cross-cultural theological education: moving the seminary out to express theological education in appropriate response to various cultural contexts and communities. Part of that experience leads faculty and administrators to questions about how we train people for ordination in a church that is changing and has been changing for some time. What skills do the newly ordained need to have? What kinds of spiritual formation will prepare them for a life of servant ministry instead of being "in charge"?

So many of the church's needs are regional and local. In meeting those needs, imagination is a more valuable gift than is a model or a set system. The ways in which an East Coast seminary addresses challenges in ministry development will—or should—differ markedly from similar issues addressed in the Middle West or the West. We have become so used to the expression "the national church," which presupposes a uniformity of context from sea to shining sea, when any denomination is a very regional church expressing a great and wonderful variety of cultures that can interact effectively with one another and with respect for one another. I do see imagination taking root in our theological education, and we can expect the seminaries to face the kind of tension that such imagination brings into a set of older systems and models that have not really dealt with a totally ministering church.

We need our scholars, and we need well-trained people to train others for continually developing ministry, but such training needs to take place with a deep respect for relationships: with the body, not *to* or even *for* the body; as part of the journeying fellowship, set within that community, rather than standing apart from it or above it. The old system has contained a valuable body of knowledge we will not want to lose or sacrifice to neosystems. But that knowledge must stimulate imagination and adventure to become great spiritual gifts on this kingdom journey.

In total-ministry development there are no better or higher expressions of ministry. There may be degrees of humility, but they arise out of social, cultural, and even personal needs and traditions. The Spirit takes our diverse gifts and coordinates a body that functions as the Spirit directs and human response allows.

CHAPTER 3

The Bishop in the Total-Ministry Context

Many good and helpful things have been written over the past several years, trying to clarify the role of bishops and other expressions of judicatory leadership as the church marches toward a new millennium. While a strong common thread runs through episcopate and similar leadership roles in other denominations, we also know that local contexts as well as personal gifts give a great deal of color and variety to such leadership roles as they are lived out.

Certainly that is true when one considers allowing the episcopate to be touched by the total-ministry process. My call to episcopacy in Nevada came with the challenge to see how total-ministry discernment could be included in and expressed by that office; in my tenure it has been gratifying to remain open to such possibilities. I speak here of my own experience because that is what I know best. But in talking with judicatory leaders in other denominations, I have learned that we travel similar roads in our responses and responsibilities.

Given our diocese's understanding of the Spirit's centrality in the ministry of the church body, the first challenge for me as bishop was to reconsider the idea of episcopal control. More and more I have seen myself not as the leader who charges out in front of his flock, always admonishing to "do more" or "be more," but as the cornerstone of ministry support and development in the diocese. In an earlier chapter I noted the question posed during the interview process for bishop: "Are you the kind of leader who rushes on ahead without looking back to see if anyone is following, or will you move along with us?"

I like the biblical image of leadership as leaven, which works within the loaf (or the lump!) to facilitate its rising, though a parishioner in one parish, a man who worked for General Mills, likened my leadership role as pastor to gluten, which helps to keep the loaf together (coordinated). Whatever images one chooses, in the context of total ministry the role of bishop is as ministry support and ministry developer. That frees me from having to come up with "my" new programs. It allows me to water with some integrity the seeds planted by my predecessor Wes Frensdorff and to rejoice in and nurture other forms of ministry life that have emerged since his time. In this context the surrender of the kind of control that rightly or wrongly has long been associated with this office is important to my understanding of the bishop's role. I really cannot prescribe for another diocese or for different denominational settings.

I had been intrigued by the concept of "shared episcopate" as friends and I had discussed it prior to my election. It is, however, a truth that one knows more about before one becomes a bishop than one may know after the fact. The practice of "shared episcopate" has eluded me, perhaps because it still has something of an air of control about it: "I'll give away this much of it so long as you realize it is mine to give." Such sharing also allows for the possibility that I can take it back when and if I want.

Extended episcopate has felt more appropriate in the Nevada context. At present I work with three regional vicars who are seminary-trained priests, and we are planning to add one more for one of our most remote areas. We understand that they are extended episcopate, in that they provide consistent teaching, training, and pastoral care; they articulate the bishop's role as leaven in the areas of their responsibility. The four of us form a collegium that shares and expresses the call to ministry support and ministry development. We meet regularly and communicate often to share the total picture of the diocese, to listen to what people are telling or showing us about their parish developments, and to offer insight and support to one another in our listening and responding to those with whom we work. We are accountable to one another and, in that, to the Spirit and the Spirit's people in this diocese.

One of the interesting lessons I have had to learn deals with what I call my "white charger syndrome," where I have felt the need to move into difficult local situations to call those involved to a righteousness that I, as bishop and pastor, can perceive. The regional vicars have been gentle but firm in convincing me that such action would create greater problems; and I have been content to let go of immediate involvement in local situations where the strong relationship between the regional vicar and the parish provides the context where growth can come out of conflict. Our strong commitment to communication, and our real friendship, allows me and the other vicars to be very aware of what is happening in thriving parishes as well as those experiencing growing pains or some other difficulty. We are not necessarily a problem-oriented group, though that element is part of the church anywhere. We also enjoy the good news of how the Spirit is working in the churches and how people are moving with that inspiration. We also see a lot of humor in this journey, and that keeps our leadership focused and open.

The removal of control as an administrative centerpiece does not preclude ordinary responsibilities. In addition to the normal canonical responsibilities that fall on a diocesan bishop, we also see the episcopal office as the focus for accountability in the diocese. Given the understanding that the definition of the judicatory or of judicatory responsibility does not lie in a hierarchical system but in the relationship of all the parishes in a geographical area, it falls to the bishop to encourage communication among parishes in the diocese and to promote the judicatory health that comes from such communication. The vicars, as extended episcopate, have been working to create greater linkage among parishes in a region; people from several parishes in central Nevada, for instance, will meet several times during the year to plan liturgy, to schedule shared licensed lay and ordained preachers, and to enjoy being together to explore common concerns and hopes.

Accountability also surfaces during "official" and unofficial episcopal visitations, when I am frequently asked to report on what is happening in other parishes: "How is Grace doing with its plan to build in the new developing part of Las Vegas?" "What is Eureka up to these days?" "How are plans going for a new vicar in the northeast region?" And so on. In that context, the focus for accountability becomes an occasion to share good news about friends and co-workers in this vast, yet closely related diocese. True, there are also losses and other sadder things to share at times, and they become the occasion for prayer long after the visitation has concluded. But, again, the focus is appropriately on our being members one with another in a visible body; the sense of accountability derives from that understanding.

Often "accountability" directs one to the disciplinary actions for clergy who have in some way stumbled and fallen or betrayed the trust placed in them, circumstances which are all too much in the news these days. I need to say three things about that. I have had to refer to those canons only some three or four times in the past nine years. Second, when a diocese is using the proper process for calling local clergy, if that process is grounded in study and prayer, those called are generally not prone to canonical offenses the likes of which are consuming so much of the church's time today. And consider this: When the Spirit moves in a small, rural town, the Spirit is moving in a place where no secrets are hid. Then third, when a diocese is committed to total ministry, those in the diocese also recognize the need for total accountability. All baptized ministers are accountable for how they "proclaim by word and example the good news of God in Christ." The continuing education process heightens that awareness among all our ministering people and grounds the church in a firm understanding of what the Good News is and who it is about!

Such definition gives considerable dimension to the episcopal role of oversight. For it is the function of the bishop to listen to and hold up the vision of the diocese's mission. The listening part is essential. It is not unlike the role of a spiritual director, who assists and nurtures growth, first by listening to those with whom the director is working. The bishop, and the extended episcopate, listens to and watches for where the Lord is working, where the Spirit may be coordinating or reforming the balance of gifts; then the bishop helps to articulate the vision so that it may be truly owned by the ministering communities in the judicatory. This also assists the bishop and the extended episcopate in the linkage role they perform throughout the diocese. (This linkage is an essential part of the job description for regional vicars as extended episcopate.)[1]

Oversight has also been expressed in how the diocese gathers around the vision to stretch the vision. Annual diocesan conventions in Nevada do not "do" resolutions. Delegates to the convention gather to do the business of the diocese (budget, special reports not published in the *Journal of Convention*, and elections). The main business of the convention is the business of God and is centered in exploring some area— ministry tools, challenges, possibilities, or opportunities—that has been identified months before the gathering and for which parishes have done appropriate, guided Bible study.[2] Topics have included: money; being good news and making it public; our vision of God; and mission (in several different perspectives). Some years feature a visiting keynoter or workshop leader; in other years we work out the possibilities before us in small groups and plenary sessions of gathered insights and concerns. The vision for oversight behind this plan for the annual judicatory gathering is to allow the church in this diocese to be encouraged in focusing on Good News, not to the exclusion of the difficulties we may face in expressing it, but with the understanding that expressing Good News *is* our task. We are not gathered—or sent forth—to be fascinated with and capitulate to bad news.

This change grew out of an awareness that old systems of parliamentary debate, together with the old angers they reveal, divide up the body, leaving its separated members feeling "more holy" and "more right" and antagonistic toward one another. We felt the need to refocus or grind the lenses through which we perceive our identity and direction, so we could discern the relationships that are the framework for the ministry of the diocesan household and, beyond that, for the ministry of the whole church in its wider, global context.

The real turning point for us came at an annual diocesan convention celebrating what it meant to be a resurrected people. Our conventions last from Friday evening until late Sunday morning when we conclude with a Eucharist. About an hour before the scheduled Eucharist, the convention all but fell apart. There were accusations that the bishop's staff was larger than it had ever been, which was not so; and the pattern of old behaviors drew a clear line between smaller, rural parishes and those in the two more developed areas of the state. So we left the convention as a fractured, rather than a truly risen, people.

In calling around to talk with some of the participants after the convention, I learned one very important thing: to confront misinformation immediately, which I had not done. This was made clear to me by one who had given out such misinformation in the heat of discussion. And I learned that we were not being as clear as we thought we were being about the nature and direction of the total-ministry development process. To clarify our direction, in subsequent years we have focused on the theme the Business of God. The next year we talked about what the business of God is, and we have continued with the vision of God that underlies that business, its expression in mission, and how we are led by the Spirit in mission. It is part of the leadership function to hold up the vision so that those who are "in it" can be clear about the context in which they live and minister.

These few paragraphs cannot hope to cover all the bishop's necessary duties or even those unnecessary ones we sometimes choose to
accept, but they can begin to reframe the context we accept for the judicatory leadership role in total ministry. There are, of course, decisions
and initiatives that remain to the episcopal office as in any judicatory
leader's experience, but they can most often be handled in consultation.
The very concept of *total* ministry challenges the "star system" that has
attended the election and treatment of bishops over the generations: the
raising up and setting apart (images of hierarchy) that deny the coordination of community that total ministry recaptures. Other denominations
have different, possibly less hierarchical, ways of electing or selecting
such leadership, but I think it is fair to say that in many of them there are
still hints and notes, if not symphonies, of hierarchy.

So in the context of total ministry, we are trying to express episcopate in terms of servant ministry, in the sense that the bishop supports the
full participation of every baptized person in the expression of Christ's
ministry within the diocese, and as much as possible beyond the diocese.
It is the bishop's responsibility to provide that sense of spiritual direction
that allows the people who are the diocese to maintain, stretch, and
sometimes refocus the diocesan vision for the ministry-to-mission, and in
that revisioning to be accountable to one another *in Christ*. Once again,
one can substitute other appropriate denominational office descriptions
for "bishop," and the principle remains the same.

One healthy spinoff of this understanding of leadership is that the old
saw about life being "lonely at the top" needn't be true of servant ministry.
The bishop can lose or even surrender the one-word title, "Thebishop"
(often used as in "Thebishopsays"), and become a friend with a first
name, a Christian name. I do not use "friend" here in the sense of "good
ol' buddy," but in the sense of those whom Jesus calls friends in John 15,
friends who are commissioned to bearing fruit, to doing together the
work they are called to do. And friends can have fun together gathered
around their common center. Of course this goes back to a repentance of
the old hierarchical systems that make impossible demands on bishops,
priests, deacons, and laity alike. The vision of total ministry as nonsys-
tematic but systemic makes that possible.

In this kind of total-ministry context, a judicatory leader can become
effectively a sign of the church's unity, because that person is a *part* of
ministry development support rather than *above* it. As sacrament of that,

I go to parishes as a *con*celebrant as often as possible, which means that I go to celebrate with a congregation and ask the local clergy to be present —seen and heard—at the altar with me during our Eucharist. This attempts to offer a picture of solidarity in shared ministry as opposed to the vision of a visiting hierarch.

Lest this description sound too facile, it needs to be said that there is also some tension in trying to live out episcopacy in total-ministry terms. Most of us who are "of an episcopal age" and have been elected to denominational leadership grew up in some entirely different systems that are still alive, if not well, and have corresponding effect on how well we readjust.

As noted elsewhere, old systems tend to resurface when one is sure they have been transformed or gone. It is my own experience that I live with and sometimes live into old ways of being a bishop—ways I thought I had forsaken. It is not unlike the new-parent boast—"I'm going to do this different from (and better than) my parents!"—and then one day to hear your parent's voice in the ways you speak to your own children.

Parent is not an apt image for episcopacy or any denominational leadership; teacher or educator or spiritual director would be better comparisons. But as in any time of change or transformation, it is hard to shed the images and imports of past generations when so many still live there and were born and grew up in the context of those images and their authorities. And authority seems to be a major concern. About every ten years, the bishops of the worldwide Anglican Communion meet in England at the invitation of the archbishop of Canterbury at what is known as the Lambeth Conference. Lambeth 1988 spent considerable time addressing authority in the church, and a great deal of energy still goes into exploring the authority of scripture. Part of the hidden agenda in these explorations seems to involve *who* has authority over whom and who defines the authority of scripture. There are still issues of control even in our most well-intentioned debates and explorations. Authority resides as well in such titles as CEO, bishop, rector, priest-in-charge, district superintendent, and conference minister. The old pyramid still rises in the desert and elsewhere, though we need to be careful in recognizing that structure is not always hierarchy. Structure is one place where hierarchy can slip in and grow in power.

The shift back to community authority hangs in complementary tension with the episcopal role as the one who listens for and helps to articulate the community-diocesan vision. And so it is that I find myself relying not only on my own intuitive and practical responses to emerging ministry issues, but submitting those responses to some kind of community reflection, usually with the regional vicars at first. That adds to the description of episcopacy the burden and the possibility of honesty: being able to admit that one is not always sure where the road is leading, being able to accept both correction and consultation along the way.

Vocabulary

Much of our difficulty in expressing total ministry as a shared expression of Christ's ministry by laity and clergy rides on the traditionally vertical nature of our ministry vocabulary. Old systems do have a way of reappearing just when we think we have moved beyond them. From time to time we still hear congregation members speak of "raising up" someone after a carefully prepared-for commendation. Indeed, the ordinal in *The Book of Common Prayer* is of little help here; the prayers that follow the Eucharist in each of the three ordination services give thanks for "raising up among us" the ordained. We find the regular post-Communion prayers in our contemporary Eucharist more suitable, especially the one which prays, "And now, Father, send *us* out to do the work you have given *us* to do" (italics mine), which puts the shared ministry of all the baptized in proper focus and keeps the job description intact for God's servant people, including the ordained among them.

CHAPTER 4

Maintenance and Mission

In chapter 1, I mentioned one visitor's perception that total ministry was a system to maintain dying churches—not conducive to the missionary enterprise of the church. That reflects the church's long-lived tension between maintenance and mission.

I would like to suggest that there is little mission that can happen without maintenance, but I do that by recasting the definition of *maintenance*. I do not take that word to mean the keeping alive of old programs that no longer work or the nurturing of old structures that imprison rather than free the members of Christ's church. *Maintenance* refers to keeping a local congregation or a diocese *centered* so that its members are sent with common purpose and energy. The calling of local clergy in more remote areas serves to keep the sacramental life of the parish alive, so that people are fed, strengthened, and renewed for the mission that is their vocation.

Sacramental maintenance need not be elaborate or complex. It means simply that the community, whatever its size, gathers around the Lord who both calls and sends them and is available to them in "the apostles' teaching and fellowship, in the breaking of bread, and in the prayers," as described in *The Book of Common Prayer* baptismal covenant. A community maintenance allows the members of the community (the body) to work together in coordinated and inspired ministry that can translate into mission.

Mission, too, has many different connotations, and we need to be careful not to write off the long-standing sense of mission as reaching out over national borders and across oceans to those in other lands. In this shrinking world, that is very much part of the church's task.

But mission also has more local ramifications in the sense of expressing Christ's ministry in a congregation's own immediate environment, in communities that are often largely unchurched. I can think of at least two fairly remote parishes whose exploration of total ministry as a lifestyle has reached out to people who are lapsed or who have had no serious previous religious affiliation; once ministry becomes shared, no small core group is doing everything and complaining about it before eventually burning out. Once ministry begins to be shared, there is more opportunity to enjoy it, even to have fun doing it. Once that mindset begins to show, curious outsiders go to see what is really happening to those folks who are actually having some fun as church! There's a strong feeling of evangelism in that.

Much attention has been given, and for good cause, to clergy burnout. I suspect we would have to admit that clergy burnout has some roots in the sense of solitary omnicompetence that has been part of the clergy job description (or myth), where ministry for everyone else is the job of the ordained person. The same issues exist, if in different flavors, for active laypeople, especially when they are involved in supermaintenance, doing things *at church* several times a week. Instead, they need to be encouraged to find ways to be *as church* in their other contexts, by discerning with the rest of the congregation or diocese those arenas where they need to be present as church in service and mission. One young man was spending at least four nights a week and time on weekends doing "church work": attending Bible study, Diocesan School of Theology classes in two different locations, repairing the church building, and being generally available to all except his family. And he wasn't even ordained! The regional vicar worked with him to reestablish priorities and to cut down on that kind of maintenance time.

Ministry and Local Identity

With that in mind, we encourage congregations to reexamine the claims the church has in former times visited upon local parishes, usually with midsized and larger congregations seen as the norm. Those claims were expressed mainly in the number of committees, commissions, and other task-specific groups that became central to congregational and diocesan life three and four decades ago. They originated in a national context and then filtered "down" to judicatory and parish levels. They did provide significant areas of involvement for people in midsized and larger parishes. But these encouragements to involvement became a burden and a frustration to smaller congregations where a few people tried to do everything. As an alternative to that in areas where the church is small and even remotely located, we ask each local parish to pray about and consider what its vocation is *in the community where the parish is called to be unique.* For instance, consider a parish in one sparsely populated area of the state that has somewhere between ten and twenty-five members. They have two local priests, who call themselves the "white-haired ladies." (A tourist passing through asked the husband of one of them, "Is that the church where the white–haired ladies are?" It stuck and continues to be a source of local merriment.) Most in the congregation tithe; they are mindful of the needs of strangers traveling through or getting lost; they have some wonderful stories to tell about wayfaring strangers. They are very much in the community as church people, and they are recognized as that by other residents. The church even provides some leadership in community events. They have no evangelism, stewardship, Christian social relations, or mission committees, but they are doing those expressions of ministry where they are as who they are. They do not spend a lot of time in church maintaining old functions. They *are* church where they live, and I would commend that as a form of mission where it is often most difficult: at home.

An example of their local leadership came several years ago, when they announced their plans for a small-scale Christmas pageant. People with other denominational backgrounds asked that they be included, and the service grew to such proportions that it had to be performed twice in the small church, with full attendance each time. No commission planned the event. The people and clergy of that parish were recognized by the community as good-news bearers. It wasn't a sustained program, but I would call it evangelism nonetheless.

Such evangelism is part of mission, and we are trying to name the good-news-as-mission task more clearly. To do that, we are taking a new look at how we describe our structures.

A number of years ago, the Diocesan Constitution and Canons were revised so that every congregation was designated a parish, eliminating the hierarchical economic systems expressed in terms of *parish, aided parish, mission,* and so forth still thriving in some parts of the Episcopal

Church. I have noted a similar shift in other denominations as well.
The intention of the change here in Nevada was to reflect the equality of
ministers in the total-ministry adventure. Aside from that good intention,
it has also made diocesan administrative tasks much easier because systems of economic discrimination create more record-keeping and clerical
office work. Now we have reached a time in our own ministry development where the term *parish* seems to lack the power and impetus we
need to feel and express. It has that old English sense of boundaries and
settledness, which has found widespread subscription in this country. It
is my hope that we will choose to designate all our congregations as
"missions" and find a way to do that without confusing ourselves with
regard to the national canons and the definitions they provide. For in a
very clear sense they are maintenance definitions that do not always
serve the purposes of mission.

There is another example of using vocabulary as an impetus to understanding the church's identity and purpose: to be a *nave* in the sense
of being a ship at sail on the sea rather than safely, and canonically,
moored in a harbor. Without damaging the metaphor too severely, we
might add that the tides of traditional vocabulary make it all the more
difficult to set sail and move out of the harbor.

Mission, especially local mission, is risky business. It demands that
a ministering community be appropriately centered and thus maintained,
so that its primary vision is of inclusive gospel rather than consumer
program appeal, with a greater emphasis on organism rather than organization. Mission does not preclude imaginative programming. A clear
understanding helps to keep that programming focused and centered on
gospel and to grow out from that awareness of Good News. Happily,
there is much evidence that such a Spirit is moving among the churches
of many denominations.

A Tale of Two Parishes/Missions

Saint Christopher's Church has had a bumpy history. Some twenty-odd
years ago, the rector found and spread a "true faith" that divided up the
congregation and locked out others (as well as the bishop). The bishop's
pastoral patience seemed to keep the situation in a necessary limbo:
those who were "absolutely right" continued in the church building while

the rest worshipped in a local community church. A fire claimed the best part of the church building a year later. At that time the diocese went to court and reclaimed the property, while the rector and a few of his flock went on to the Roman Catholic Church.

A new rector came on board and managed considerable healing, though he was constantly confronted by those few in the parish who knew exactly how everything should be done, with some partisan advice from outside the parish.

When I arrived as bishop, the parish was once again divided. A part-time supply priest and a lay member of the parish, an attorney, were at war over some churchmanship issues, focusing at first on the use of the 1928 *Prayer Book* and then fanning out into more personal issues. The battle was even being waged in the parish newsletter, with some obvious pastoral fallout and distress.

An intervention was called for, and took place, pleasing neither of the antagonists. The priest was asked to limit his Sunday visits to the parish and to avoid comment on the divisive situation. After an attempt to tone down the attorney's behavior, it became necessary to withdraw his lay reader's license until the conflict could be resolved. No one was happy about those intermediate steps. Two priests were assigned to assist the parish in its healing: one a diocesan staff regional vicar and the other a seminary-trained woman with considerable pastoral skills. Over the next year of training and caring, total-ministry issues were explored and explained; the ministry of all the baptized became both focus and invitation in the ministry studies led by the regional vicar. Pastoral care was provided in the sense of listening to people's pains and angers and helping people move on from such preoccupations.

At my next annual visit, the entire parish came singly for the reaffirmation of the baptismal covenant, one by one to acknowledge obedience to the promises made in baptism and to receive support from others and to offer the same to one another as a ministering community. That was maintenance with momentum.

It was a very moving service, but not so moving as what happened subsequently. After appropriate study and prayer, the parish called from among them a deacon and, a year later, a priest. Both have since been ordained, but the parish's vision of ministry did not wait for the ordinations. With strong lay leadership, the parish began and invited other denominations to join in a ministry of respite care for people in the community burdened with the care of ailing spouses or aged parents. The deacon, who is also a nurse, worked with an experienced social worker in the parish to organize volunteer training. The United Thank Offering, gathered and administered nationally by the Episcopal Church Women, provided a start-up grant, and the program took off. That mission to the community and *with* the community has continued to grow in scope and effect in a city that needed such a ministry. Saint Christopher's *listened* to the needs of the community in which it has been called to serve and witness, and then it *trained and moved,* being responsive to that call to local mission.

That involvement has not dampened their concerns for wider mission opportunities in the diocese and beyond. It has made the church far more visible in its own place. I was having a meal at a local restaurant on one occasion, and the waiter asked which church I "worked at." When I responded, "Episcopal," he said, "Oh, that's the church that cares about the shut-in people and their families!" Not a bad witness, I'd say.

Grace-in-the-Desert is a newer parish, about five years old. An emerging missionary community, it began with a priest hired to plant a new church in a given area. The priest had special training in church growth. They began worship in a local YMCA. Their "stained glass window" was a very large mural on a concrete block wall—a woman engaged in some aerobic activity. They used nontraditional music well done on a good sound system, and an overhead projector conveyed to the new congregation the unfamiliar words of the liturgy; only a few had any experience of the Episcopal Church. The parish's intent had been to reach out to the unchurched, and it did that and continues in that outreach. The model for church growth in which the priest had been trained really did not work as well as hoped in this particular area, and other personal difficulties saw the priest's departure and a reduction in an already small membership.

Some five families hung on, and, through their persistence and witness, the parish has continued to grow. A move to a preschool facility made them more visible, and they have purchased land in a rapidly growing planned community. But from the very beginning their vision has been to serve the community, not just to build a church. This has grown from one of the basic principles of the newly forming congregation: that this church would "have babies"—become a training center for mission in the area.

Seeing the number of young families in their new neighborhood, they plan to begin their building project with a preschool facility, which may also serve as worship space, the idea being that worship can happen where service is being offered. That early vision is a sign of the way the congregation looks outward to the possibilities for mission where it is. There is much to do and a lot to grow. They have called and I have ordained two for priesthood and one for deacon, understanding their twin needs for sacramental centering and worship and the importance of listening for and acting upon the vocation to serve the Lord where he is to be found.

They are looking ahead as well to the possibility of a day-care center for the elderly as they build and equip the church facility. To date these are visions rather than concrete realities, but the visions are rooted in a kind of sacramental centeredness that makes the worshipping community a ministering community at the same time.

Neither of these two parishes is doing anything utterly new, but they both represent a sense of leadership style markedly different in emphasis from what has been offered to them by older generations. Leadership is not assigned by (holy) order, but it is transferrable and flexible. It can be passed around as the occasion and the vocation may require. For example, those called for ordination were real leaders in the small parish of Grace-in-the-Desert, serving on its vestry and organizing much of the parish's life. Upon ordination, they remain leaders still, but they have passed on the formal leadership roles to others as the parish grows rapidly. This understanding of leadership allows for a degree of spontaneity in response and planning that has not always characterized the church's sense of its own mission. It is cooperative, often lay initiated, and shared among people in community who may be laity or clergy. In that cooperative sense, it has that air of being *coordinated* by the Spirit, and it is in the power of the Spirit that we move as a spiritually and sacramentally maintained body into mission.

A Helpful Dynamic

In the fall of 1994, I attended a conference in Seattle. Our purpose was to form a new multicultural commission to replace the separate ethnic entities that had been functioning on the Episcopal Church's national level. I was attending as an outgoing member of the Episcopal Commission on

Indian Ministry (ECIM). At the conference the four different ethnic groups (Afro-American, Asiamerican, Hispanic, and Native American) were to meet separately for the first two days to prepare for their coming together for planning ways to express this new shared identity.

The ECIM group—all Native Americans except me—met in a board room at the top of the Seattle Hilton and began as we always did—with Eucharist, not the hurry-up kind that is focused on the agenda to follow, but a time of centering, of remembering whose we are. Following the Eucharist was "check-in time," when the twelve or so people were asked to tell what joys had been part of their lives since we last met. We all spoke and listened to one another, so that by the time we got to "business," the long board room table had become round. Sacramental centeredness and caring fellowship, both maintenance functions, made us ready to look at our part in the mission to God's whole church; it was a very creative meeting with real action to take place as we dispersed.

The Role of the Ordained

In this understanding of the maintained and mission-focused community—the ministering community—the role of the ordained becomes clear. The priest becomes the maintenance person, the temple person. The priest gathers the community for its sacramental life, for the feeding and energizing that is central to the ministering community. The priest is the gatherer around a center who is *not* the priest, but the Lord whom we all worship. The priest points the people toward the center. The priest is not the center, a truth which we continue to discover in our total-ministry explorations and adventures. We use Wes Frensdorff's distinction that the church is a ministering community rather than a community gathered around a minister.

The function of the deacon is to encourage and help train the ministering community for mission. Our eucharistic liturgy concludes with a dismissal, a go-forth-to-serve direction, given by the deacon when one is present. The dismissal serves as a constant reminder that maintenance has momentum and is directed to mission. Our challenge is to remember that and to resist the old temptations to get our own house in order and then relax and enjoy it. That is not true maintenance. It is the avoidance of vocation. True maintenance centers the ministering community and motivates it to do mission.

CHAPTER 5

New Twists on "Downsizing" and "Upsizing"

The vertical imagery of the church's language has not always been as helpful or even as diagnostic as some have accepted and believed. A current and questionable preoccupation with gain or loss of membership has hatched these new terms for describing our life together: *downsizing* to describe loss, or, in areas where membership is increasing, the more optimistic *upsizing*. They may be offered partly as "reality" for where the church is in the world these days, or as an excuse for a dear but ailing friend or an encouragement to one who is recovering. Old associations die slowly and with difficulty. *Down* still means "not-so-good, failing," or at worst "failure." *Up* can mean "growing, succeeding," even "success." I do not believe that those who offer these terms operate fully out of such a context, but of course what is said and what is heard and appropriated often differ markedly.

A Garden Metaphor

There are creative possibilities in this vertical imagery, especially in agricultural imagery. Going "down" might include digging down to reexamine the roots of vocation in biblical context and in a specific place, by asking some radical questions: "Why are we here? How are we called to be here? How are we called to grow? What is the soil in which we are planted telling us, nourishing us to do?"

Asking such questions might lead to some judicious pruning, trimming off the suckers and other nonproductive growths that sap the energy of the plant and use the root's energy to no avail. Paring down may well assist a congregation or a diocese in reordering priorities and sacrificing preoccupations and institutional claims that have neither served the kingdom of God nor been particularly good news in its own "garden plot."

Going "up" might suggest how we wonder about where we are supposed to stretch, to branch out, to adapt to the environment in which we are called to be good news. In our small desert vegetable garden, we have noticed how the early string bean leaves grow at a ninety-degree angle to the sun in the heat of the day, so they do not get scorched. Then, in our back yard, the fig tree has broad, heavy and tough, leaves. Similarly, the church grows in different ways in different places; it is stretched not by universal formulae, but by the particulars of the garden or vineyard in which it is planted.

So it can be said that for the church *up* and *down* often can look quite alike in terms of being helpful directions. I mentioned earlier how it has been necessary to reconsider institutional claims and organizations developed in and before the 1950s: the often very effective committees and commissions and task forces that offered some focus and direction for the church's life and mission in earlier decades. As these structures became well established, they also seemed to lose a sense of critical self-examination and instead just went on, propelled mostly by a historical momentum. In turn, they became burdens for loyal church people in smaller congregations and dioceses. People burned out trying to live up to and into obligations that no longer served a mission with which they could identify. Giving up this committee or that commission did provide some guilty feelings along the way, but the resulting freedom to readapt ministry and the mission that ministry serves began to offset the "we no longer have" or "we no longer do" syndromes with a renewed and reclaimed sense of baptismal ministry *in this place*. The Episcopal Church in Nevada has had to reexamine its roots, to reconsider the environment in which it is called to be church. New forms of ministry have been recognized and old expressions of ministry, forgotten for a time, have emerged once again. That's creative "going down," looking to where we are planted and acknowledging the character of the soil in which we are to grow.

New "Shoots"

One example of such creative downsizing is found in the current status of the Episcopal Church Women organization. In some of our parishes, the women still meet regularly and conduct the business that has for so long been important to the worldwide mission of the church in support of foreign and domestic missionaries and educating local parishes about mission *beyond* the parish. But with more women employed full-time and considering the vastness of our diocese and attendant travel problems, a diocesan-wide expression of the Episcopal Church Women is increasingly frustrating. A few women have met to discuss the future of this loosely knit organization and to develop a new perspective for the essential work of women in the church and as the church. The new designation will be something like Nevada Episcopal Women in Ministry. Plans are developing for annual regional meetings to explore and share the many ways in which women express vocation. That is still in the more-to-come stages, but it promises to be another contribution to our understanding and development of total ministry.

Another example is the emergence of the lay preacher. In areas where full-time, seminary-trained clergy are not economically feasible, the Word still needs to be preached. So we have recognized and trained people who are gifted in sharing the good news of God in Christ in this particular way. These are people who speak the language of the land in which they serve and are recognized as finding and sharing where the Word of God is in that language and in this land. That is one way of expressing downsizing from an older system that no longer works in this garden. I hesitate to carry the image further and describe it as a process of fertilization because of the other associations that may recall; but it is a way of feeding the garden where we are planted now, so that it can upsize or be stretched.

So we see a lay preacher from one parish traveling anywhere from an hour-and-a-half to three hours to another parish to share the Word. In that there is a sense of linkage and solidarity that pulls the diocese together in creating community beyond the town limits.

Knowing the Soil

It is helpful to learn from history why "downsizing" happens and where it can lead. The smaller, more rural churches in this diocese began to downsize years ago as mines closed and people moved away. Ours has sometimes been called a boom-or-bust economy, and to some degree that has affected the life of the church. The people went away when their places of employment closed. Some stayed, however, and so the church stayed—perhaps smaller, somewhat depressed at first, but open to staying alive in new circumstances. These are hardy churches, no matter what their size.

It was this ecclesiastical climate that received the "new" idea of local clergy—clergy called from the congregation as nonstipendiary, to keep the sacramental life of the parish alive. This was not accomplished quickly. Training was careful and extended. The first such ordinations occurred in 1979, when three were ordained to the transitional diaconate and to priesthood the following year. The first local deacon was ordained in 1982, and the records indicate a slow progress as congregations became ready to call clergy from their own midsts and struggled to understand the difference from full-time, paid rectors. The process was not without some pain, as noted earlier in these pages. But good things have happened and are there to instruct us in the values of what is called "downsizing."

Is This Downsizing?

Christ Church lives in a small town near the Utah border—one of those towns where the mine closed some years ago. This parish was one of the first to call a local priest. Laypeople have taken the major responsibility in organizing the life of the parish, allowing their priest to be both priest and friend. While there are several other denominations in town, Christ Church has become something of a community church. Last year it hosted the community Christmas Eve service, led by laypeople because the priest was away with her husband visiting family. Community youth have gathered for programs here and then attended the diocesan camp without fuss or bother about what church they really belong to. Without giving place to denominational competition, Christ Church has become leaven in the Christian community and encourager of ecumenical sharing. It is not a big church, but there are new faces in the congregation as people move into the area; there is a big spirit among those who gather here in Christ's name.

A like theme appears in a different way in Saint Francis' Church, located in another area where mines have closed and years of drought have taken their toll. The people of Saint Francis and the local Methodist church began to worship together more than twenty years ago—one Sunday in the Methodist church and the next Sunday in the Episcopal church. Sometimes served by visiting Episcopal or Methodist clergy, they developed a close and friendly relationship—to the extent that when one temporary pastor sought to return the Methodists to a more rigorous denominational position, the Methodists objected that he was breaking up the family, meaning their relationship with the Episcopal sisters and brothers!

Several years ago, the difficult decision was made to meet in one place every Sunday. Too many people had fallen through the cracks in the weekly building switch. The size and facility of the Methodist church made it the logical choice, and some of the Episcopalians began to grieve the "loss" of their building. The resident priest, paid for partly by the two congregations and partly by the diocese, saw this as an opportunity for community program; the Episcopal church building became a place for weekly luncheons for mothers with small children, scout meetings, and other such gathering activities. Other ecumenical service programs such as food and clothing banks evolved as members of the church learned to move out from the building into the community. While there is some individual resistance still to this new face for the church, the strength of ecumenical worship becoming ecumenical service is dramatic.

It is not a picture of organic unity, however. Some old systems remain. The Episcopalians pay their allotment to the diocese, and the Methodists are expected to do the same in their district, so there are two collections each Sunday. There are two cups as well; the Episcopal chalice with wine, and the Methodist cup with grape juice. This element does not seem to be a distraction. It even has its holy humorous moments. The present priest was ordained to that office in the Methodist church where the two congregations meet together. The Methodist district superintendent preached and joined me at the altar and administered the cup with grape juice, while a layperson administered the "Episcopal" cup containing wine. As the time of Communion progressed, there was a considerable line of Methodists receiving from the cup of wine, while the Episcopal clergy present and vested ended up receiving grape juice. It was an ecumenical test, and everyone passed!

The most interesting development has been the growth in membership involving people who are neither Episcopalian nor Methodist, but who have some other vague or historical connection to yet another denomination. Rather than to force those people into a denominational box, the church has welcomed them as who they are, as baptized members. Like Christ Church above, they are fast becoming a community church with a rotating Episcopal-Methodist liturgy. The worship is not a problem so long as people can express their identity as Christian instead of a common denominational label. That seems to be a very prophetic lifestyle for a church in a small community that is beginning to grow once again as mining returns to the area.

Other churches in the diocese reflect the same kind of direction in terms of increased ecumenical cooperation and sharing. This development is leading us to recognize the work of the coordinating Spirit in our midst. In conversations with friends who are judicatory representatives in the United Methodist and Lutheran (ELCA) churches, we are trying to commit to a reluctance to "build our own thing" in smaller communities, and to find ways to work and worship more closely together. There is an additional concern for good stewardship in such a commitment. It is not yet a strong agreement, but it is encouraging to feel the push toward such cooperation and mutual commitment. One exciting and rewarding development for us has been the willingness of a Lutheran pastor to serve as interim regional vicar for us in the remote northeastern region. Having formerly served in part of that area as a Lutheran bishop's deputy, he brings pastoral skills for allowing people to build realistic visions of their mission. At the same time he affirms in the small communities the need for ecumenical sharing in ministry. What a blessing that has been to us and to them.

So we can say that in one way downsizing has led to an openness to other faith communities, where denominational competition is being transformed into a new kind of cooperating and living together. If this progress continues, it will cause difficulties in the ways we define our business: the statistics, systems for denominational support, even liturgical expressions. But it will also offer some fresh promise about our shared faith journey and provide a witness others need to see.

At the present time the three denominations are supporting a combined outreach to a valley outside one of our cities. Called the ELM (Episcopal, Lutheran, Methodist) Church, it began as an idea in conversations among judicatory representatives. They handed a more developed process over to three downtown churches to sponsor and oversee. As the new congregation has formed and met, it has had its identity tensions: whether to be a traditional, in-place church or a missionary outreach; what kind of worship to use; how to identify with the sponsoring denominations; how to define and support its mission. These tensions come essentially from old systems that are not going to work in this situation. The challenge now is to pray for and find the imagination to ask newer questions and move beyond old expectations. That is what the church might call "dangerous living" because it relies more heavily on the Spirit's agenda than our own. And has church planting arrived at that level of trust? I'm not convinced. But I mention that challenge in this context, because it might be considered a kind of creative downsizing in the sense of getting back to the roots of our faith and our vocation. I see this as more than the old "community church" model. It is a sense of becoming more a community than we have allowed ourselves to be, by stretching beyond borders and boundaries that are not really life giving or growth producing. This kind of ecumenical openness is a renewed commitment to the oneness and unity expressed in the high priestly prayer of John 17, which can be—but need not be—seen as a threat to denominational systems.

So far in our ELM experience, we see that each denomination has rich traditions that enhance those of others, and that we have much to share with and learn from one another without any sense of "deserting" our own denominational heritages. This is an appropriate context in which to be stretched, however, and that can be uncomfortable.

Another Kind of Sizing

Saint Stephen's is doing something different. Here a long-term rector was followed by a very short-term rector. Some people left because of the new rector; others left when and because he did. The particulars are not pertinent here, but the parish was left with reduced numbers, a reduced budget, and reduced confidence.

And they chose to face into healing. They called a local priest who had been part of the congregation for a number of years, and they also called a local deacon. They contracted with a mental health professional who is a seminary-trained priest to assist in the sacramental life of the parish. And they began to look at ministry as a parish.

They began in the right place. Instead of rushing to call clergy, they looked at themselves and asked, "What gifts do we have for ministry as this parish?" They did something I am sure many other parishes have done—putting up big signs around the parish hall representing different areas of ministry gifts. Some appropriate education prefaced the congregation's exposure to these open lists; then people were invited to identify where their gifts might be used well. The symbolism of the process was good: This all happened in *one* room. There was no mistaking that these gifts were to be coordinated in one ministry.

As their process continued, they arrived at the place where they decided not to call a salaried priest as rector. It was more than a wise budgetary decision. It was essentially a reevaluation of their vocation as a parish. Once they began to feel some momentum in their newer understanding of ministry, they worked with a regional vicar in deepening that understanding and then preparing for a commendation process for local clergy. Two members were commended for priesthood and began the process of studying and training for that with a significant number of others in the parish. One has been ordained priest and the other is moving ahead and should be ordained within the next year. At the same time, several other people are preachers-in-training, so that there are now five lay and ordained people who can preach the Word on Sunday morning. That leads to the promise, "If you don't like the sermon this Sunday, come back next week for a different preacher!" Notwithstanding that promise, the level of preaching has been very good indeed and the response enthusiastic.

From the beginning, at the healthy center of this process has been a commitment to the spirituality of the parish vocation; they have had regular parish and vestry retreats—actually going away to reflect on their life together and where they are being led. I suspect this accounts for the energy level in the parish and the attraction it holds for newcomers. There is also a commitment to sharing their gifted preachers with other, smaller congregations. This indicates they are also looking beyond their own walls.

If there is any problem in the ministry development of this parish, it may be in that same energy level. There are a lot of busy people in the parish, including a few who get too busy in their enthusiastic involvement. At the same time, I think there is a keen awareness of the need to keep focusing and refocusing these energies to avoid burnout and to express ministry effectively. Saint Stephen's is really reshaping the ministry of the parish and will provide encouragement to others who may wish to explore new coordinations in ministry. I sense they may discover a new sense of how mission is coordinated in the body of Christ in order to stretch the body outward.

As with any time of transition, there are also conflicts and misunderstandings that need to be addressed, and some members have been distressed by a kind of conflict that is essentially healthy because it is out in the open. In changing from the perceived control style of a full-time rector, control was assumed by the vestry with the best intentions of coordinating the life and the ministry of the parish. Some decisions were made that others felt needed more discussion by the entire parish. Painful things were said and heard. Their regional vicar has kept pointing out that this is a healthy process because they are talking directly to one another about it in open forum, not muttering in private corners or over the telephone. As part of this process, old wounds and griefs that most people thought had been healed began to surface. Old systems do crop up even when we think they have been put to rest. In the midst of these growing pains, the lay leadership is making a significant effort to improve communication levels, by publishing vestry minutes and announcing the time and place of each meeting, by encouraging people to be a part of these discussions and to read, mark, and inwardly digest the information provided for them. So this undertaking becomes more than a communication exercise. It addresses the need for respect in relationships, which is essential to coordinated parish ministry; that in turn allows the people in the parish to look at the alternative to being "in charge" as they remember the call to servant ministry.

What are we learning from Saint Stephen's experience? The means for doing ministry can change according to the needs and personality of a parish. It takes some courage, the ability to confess one's own sins honestly, and a willingness to let some people go elsewhere, to move out of old models and into a fresh journey; but as long as the new momentum is centered in the Spirit of God, it remains healthy and challenging and

liable to growth. It has room for mistakes, which are sometimes the keys
that unlock new possibilities. It has the capacity for channeling ministry
energy into mission strength. That is still ahead for Saint Stephen's, but
they have chosen a bold adventure and a trustworthy Friend with whom
to travel. It is not an easy journey or an easy transition, by any means.
People feel hurt, but people also forgive; and forgiveness given and
received has an uncanny way of stretching the vision of the whole
community.

Conflict and vision, faith and difficulty, anger and hope—all are
parts of this movement into the development of total ministry, which
calls upon the capacity of any given parish or diocese to be strong
enough to hang in there and keep on listening.

Saint Mary's Church lives in a small city on Interstate 80, the major
east-west route across the country's northern tier. The parish has no
building of its own, the old church having been sold a number of years
ago and now serving as a local museum. The church as people is hardly
a museum, however. They met in a Missouri Synod Lutheran church for
a number of years, until a change in Lutheran clergy made a move necessary. Then the local Roman Catholic priest welcomed them into that
parish's chapel. Worship is central for the people of Saint Mary's; visiting clergy come once or twice a month for Eucharist, and lay leaders
provide Morning Prayer on the other Sundays. But their worship has
body to it, in that it moves out into the community. Members of the parish are active in community service in any number of ways. The parish
is recognized as Saint Mary's Episcopal Church because of how members minister in the community and not because of what their building
looks like. This is certainly another kind of "sizing": a church without
walls or the preoccupations of building maintenance; their goal is not to
put up another edifice but to grow in expressing ministry where they live
and work.

A Sadder Story

Downsizing is not always creative or even voluntary. One parish in-
vested a great deal of energy in calling a stipendiary seminary-trained
priest from another diocese to help them grow and move into a firmer
sense of total ministry than their own traditions and circumstances had

allowed. It looked like a marriage made in heaven. New energy, new members, new organization bloomed where there previously had been a real or imagined nineteenth-century-type priestly control. The few rumblings I heard seemed inconsequential in the face of the visible achievements in the parish. I should have listened more carefully, for what was happening was another version of control systems. The priest was "doing for" the congregation and beginning to sound frustrated that they didn't "sign up to help" at various duties. A bare year-and-a-half later, she made the decision to leave, telling me and the congregation only after having secured another position elsewhere. The members of the congregation were hurt and angry, and their situation was aggravated further by the sense that this was the first priest they had really called by themselves, with support from the bishop and the regional vicar—and it had failed! "Failure" is a feeling more than a fact here, but the feeling rushed in to describe unmet expectations.

The resulting depression has been severe and is only slowly showing signs of recovery. One of the most tragic signals being sent by what appeared to be emerging leadership is the plaint, "I really don't know what this is about; I did it for *her*!" No one can accuse the now-absent priest of deliberately setting out to harm or mislead that congregation. Far from it. Her gifts were and are many, and her intentions were honorable. But old control systems have a way of sneaking in and being accepted, especially when it looks like "nurturing the family." That causes harm to those called to be and express the ministry of the baptized.

Going Up

Several of our urban parishes have been upsizing, showing some growth as their community population has grown. Such population increases in the city also give rise to social problems, and some of the parishes are finding that they need to devote more of their energy beyond the parish— yet *as* the parish in the community.

Christ Church is a healthy example of that. A fairly traditional parish with a sound catholic liturgical style and active program, Christ Church has a rector, one local priest, a seminary-trained assistant priest, and two locally called deacons.

The deacons are the key to ministry outreach, with unquestioned

support from the rector. When the homeless population began to swell in
the city, one of the deacons worked with laypeople and other clergy to
begin an emergency shelter in one of our smallest local parishes. A food
bank, somewhat like a minimart for the hungry, was opened in a former
classroom that faced out to the parking lot. Lines form there five days a
week. Every person is treated with dignity and respect as volunteers try
to meet their needs and those of their families. One of the deacons was
responsible for the ministry start-up, but it is entirely staffed by laypeople from Christ Church and another city parish, while still other
parishes contribute food for distribution.

Both deacons are actively involved in a new venture, remodeling an
old motel into single residence occupancy for people who are homeless
and reentering the work force. A member of the diocesan staff serves on
the board, which is now ecumenical and community-based in representation. The parish does not need to work alone in meeting needs in the
city.

One of the deacons has extensive experience in the banking field,
and she is among several people exploring new ways of using our money
to help the poor: whether through a credit union, minority-focused bank,
or through other forms of service in the community, we do not yet know.
But the energy is there to move into yet another area of local mission as
timing and wisdom allow.

The parish also has taken a considerable risk in buying a complex
of medical offices adjacent to its property. As medical and dental personnel retire and move, new service opportunities are put in place, so far
a dental clinic (with equipment donated by a retiring dentist), staffed by
volunteer dentists, and a teen clinic, managed and staffed by professionals outside the parish, that provides basic health care and counseling.
These kinds of service outreach into the community rarely stay "Episcopal," though the initiative has come from there. We are learning that
initiative need not become ownership—ours—but can more effectively
lead to partnership. We may sacrifice some public relations points in
that, but it feels consistent with our understanding of total ministry as
including *all* the baptized. It continues our sense of mission leadership
as being leaven in the community instead of celebrating only our own
piece of the "loaf."

Interestingly enough, Christ Church parish continues to grow
modestly, and some of that growth has been attracted by the parish's

visibility in the community, as members do the work God has given them to do. Newcomers enjoy the fun the parish has at various functions, as well as the sincerity and reverence of its worship. And many people become directly or tangentially involved in the reaching out of the parish to the community. Upsizing, as we see it here and in several other parishes, stretches the parish's capacity for and commitment to outreach. The downside of this upsizing is that stewardship commitments do not always keep pace with the expressions of servant ministry, so there is the constant need to look for support to keep things going. And as in any city we continue to face the problems of personal mobility, as people move in and out in considerable numbers. The challenges to creative servant ministry always seem greater than people's capacity to support it. In this facet of total-ministry development, we continue to search for ways to address this gap and educate people in stewardship response.

Being Tempted and Being Truth

Whenever we talk about size (going up or going down), we can be tempted to subscribe to a metaphor left over from old systems, especially as we talk about the capacity of a parish or a judicatory for mission, for stretching beyond where we are now. The temptation is a subtle replay of the old "charity begins at home" excuse, and it shows itself in a need to "get our own house in order," before moving into any further commitments. I believe that leads to a dead end, largely because it is self-serving and untruthful. Once one's "own house is in order" the greatest temptation is to relax and enjoy it and give the greatest effort and energy to keeping that new but old system alive. The scenario leads to being a "successful" church, when success or getting one's own house in order should be a very low priority.

If we accept, as noted earlier, that truth lies in being in relationship to Jesus Christ, then truth somehow also lies in being with him on *his* journey. The biblical witness is hardly about the kinds of security that sometimes masquerade as ecclesiastical success. Indeed, the story of the religious establishment that becomes part of the story of Jesus is a warning about becoming self-satisfied, self-preoccupied, and even self-righteous. The risks Jesus takes with tradition, with "decency and good order," in order to heal and proclaim the kingdom of God are definitive

of the spirit of mission. By comparison, our risks with structures and
ecclesiastical offices and burgeoning tradition seem small indeed. And
yet we must continue to offer these risks as resistances to the temptations
to buy into other criteria for "success."

In our tradition, to be truthful is to maintain that relationship with a
present Lord. We do Eucharist, in real presence, in worship; that gift
strengthens us to be eucharistic in our living and doing after worship.
That living and doing becomes ministry imagination in action. Ministry
imagination is simply imaging the one with whom we walk and whom
we try to serve, to the best of our ability and in the context of our membership one with another.

The necessary and helpful ambiguity in this ministry style is two-
fold. It resides in the mystery of the present Christ and how God works
through the Holy Spirit; there is no adequate formula to specify that
divine activity. It is the mystery of faith. And the ambiguity also lies in
not knowing where ministry stops and living begins: How much of our
"normal" day-to-day enterprise is witness to the living Lord, whether or
not we choose to call it ministry? As I have noted earlier, I do not believe it is necessary to catalog everything as "ministry," in order to fit
into a neat system. There is nothing particularly neat about mission.
Some of our sloppiest efforts yield fruit a hundredfold, while best laid
plans become sore spots on our collective conscience.

Once again, we feel dangerously ambiguous when we let go of control and let the Spirit be in charge. That provides all kinds of modern
tensions in the face of Careful Planning, Effective Leadership, Management Style, Significant Systems, and so on—those acceptable virtues that
somehow get elevated to positions that are way out of proportion to the
grace in which we stand, and the endurance, character, and hope with
which that gracious relationship endows the body of believers.

In terms of our discussion of church upsizing and downsizing, this
absence of needing control leads us into a deeper level of listening in
prayer and to the myriad ways in which God can speak to us. And God's
word to us may lead us into risks and adventures for which we feel un-
ready or for which others will criticize us—What else is new? Whose
kingdom are we about anyway?

CHAPTER 6

Developments, Difficulties, and Possibilities

Continuing Education

Christian education is key to effective and healthy total ministry. As noted earlier, Christian education is a necessary and life-long commitment for every baptized person, and to a large degree it is a community exercise rather than a solo expedition.

In our diocese we encourage people in a congregation to study together and geographically close congregations to study with one another, placing the call to community in education ever before us. Some people, more motivated to explore on their own, are encouraged to share their personal explorations with their congregation or region. This can create or "surface" teachers. While we do have duly licensed catechists, we are also finding laity and clergy who have teaching gifts and the education to give substance to those gifts. We also rely on seminary-trained personnel to take some leadership in this educational part of our life together.

Theological teaching and learning occur in a variety of contexts: the parish, the Diocesan School of Theology, preachers-in-training classes taught regionally, and so on. But underlying each educational context is the understanding that every Christian is a theologian. Too much emphasis has been placed on expertise in theology as a specific discipline. Necessary and essential as that is in our tradition, it ought not to obscure the fact and the obligation that every Christian talks about God. How we talk about God and about God's self-revelation is theology. How we talk about God's works is theology. It is the function of Christian education on any level to produce sound theology in the ways we talk about God.

Eric, one of our regional vicars, brought our diocese a fresh understanding of educational principles, and he has retrained us to appreciate a participatory education and deeper learning experience. In our classes we now try to include four basic areas for learning: (1) some didactic material, to get basic facts and contexts in order; (2) a "microscope" approach to deal specifically with one or two aspects of the material; (3) a "right-brain" activity, which releases another kind of imagination into the learning process; (4) discussions of how these considerations affect and touch our spiritual journey.

There is, of course, some flexibility in the balance of these four areas in any given class session. The right-brain activity might give way to a longer exploration of personal spiritual journey, or the implications of the material under study for spiritual journey may be deferred to a later class. The overall picture for a given course includes all four areas as essential.

One session of a study of Mark's Gospel might focus on the progression of chapter 1 as a process for growth in ministry: from baptism through temptation, to owning a sense of direction to the kingdom of God, then on to forming a community and healing. As a part of that study, we might note the resistance to healing that occurs in 1:24-26 in the man with an unclean spirit. A silent meditation or guided visualization on a part of Mark 1 may follow, which in turn produces a level of discussion and reflection that would not have been possible in a purely academic exercise.

Another study of a prophet's troubling journey might focus on one or two appropriate issues and be followed by a short period for the class to go outdoors and run around the block, to capture the sense of Elijah's flight in 1 Kings 19. The resulting discussion becomes profound.

One of the vicars uses paper midrash as a right-brain activity that evokes excellent theological reflection. For paper midrash, provide paper of varying colors and textures and glue sticks—that's all. Ask participants to use these resources to express nonverbal theological responses to a text and then to share them with one another.

Another class might be studying the Corinthian letters, focusing on some of the specific difficulties the Corinthian church faced. This class could be sent into groups to design a "General Convention for the Church in the First-Century Mediterranean" at which some of these concerns are addressed.

There are so many possibilities for living theological education in which learning becomes more than "ought to know"; it becomes "want to know." I see that as a healthy transition from duty to desire, from "I have to" or "we must" (how I tire of that in preaching!) to "I want to" or "we enjoy this." That forms a far more sound basis for a relationship to the One who is truth than does a sole sense of obligation. That sense of wanting and enjoyment also has a lot to do with the quality of loving. This commitment to, and enjoyment in, continuing education is one of the most encouraging trends we see in total-ministry development.

I remember a person coming to see me about a call to priesthood. Actually it was presented as a call to seminary, and it emerged as a desire once again to "know more" about God and the church. I sent him back to his own parish to reflect with friends there on his call. Some months later he returned and happily announced he was already doing theology and ministering; and he had discovered that in the context of his own community, with whom he was now engaged in a study program. He could continue to learn in that context, and he has.

Wherever we are, theological study and imagination have a place. And wherever we are is where we are needed to be theologians. We do need those who have devoted focused study to help us along the way, but it remains a cooperative rather than a hierarchical enterprise. We do not need to be asking questions about who knows more than whom but about how theology is expressed where we are as a way of ministering and of doing mission.

Difficulties

There are some obvious difficulties in maintaining a consistent under-standing of this cooperative theological enterprise.

One of the most recurrent ones lies in the mobile nature of our society. New people move into the area and have no idea what the Episcopal Church in Nevada is up to; they long for the old systems and models they have left behind.

For some time we were ignorant of their need—and our problem. But parishes have become more intentional and more careful in introducing to newcomers our sense of total ministry. We have even begun to see newcomers to the diocese appear at the Diocesan School of Theology with the intent of walking alongside us to understand and become part of this expression of Christian ministry. One new family was so curious

they enrolled each in a different class for one six-week term. Their participation disclosed gifts in ministry that they brought with them, and they
are now part of the ministry fabric in the city where they live.

The same difficulty arises in welcoming seminary-trained clergy
into our diocese. We have not had a good history in helping clergy from
outside the diocese adapt to this sense of community ministry and "real
theology." Old systems and models come in through that door, and we
have had to design a process for incorporating clergy that is more extensive than that for laity. This may be because clergy often carry more
baggage and because they are still greeted by a number of expectations
for omnicompetence. We do not have a steady flow of clergy in and out,
so we have had some time to reflect and work out a way of incorporating
them.

The diocesan commission on ministry has approved a process that
begins before any search starts. First, the bishop visits with the church
vestry or other appropriate group to outline the process, which begins
with a parish portrait that says nothing about the former rector or the one
to be called, but describes the mission of the parish and the kinds of
ministry that arise from that. After such a portrait is put together, commission members from the area meet with the vestry or, after discussion
with the bishop, commission the bishop to discuss the portrait. Once the
appropriate good-byes to the departing clergy have taken place, names of
clergy candidates are given by the bishop to the parish search committee
which has no more than two vestry members on it. When the committee
decides on one or two candidates, once again the bishop and area members of the commission on ministry meet with the candidate(s) to interpret our understanding of total-ministry development. The question I
now know I must ask is "Are you trainable?" Some are and some are
not; some know it and some do not.

Once a person has been called and is in place, a series of regular
"appointments" are scheduled with him or her by the bishop and the
commission on ministry. A new clergyperson is asked to attend one or
two diocesan commission on ministry meetings a year and diocesan
council and standing committee meetings, to get a feel for how we work
together and support one another. Meetings with the bishop and local
commission members occur at designated intervals. In the case of a parish rector, similar meetings are scheduled for the vestry, with the hope
that little (or big) things don't get suppressed for later explosion *and* that

appropriate affirmations are being given. Encouragement needs a far more prominent place on our ecclesiastical agenda.

Encouragement and Impatience

The most obvious difficulty, of course, is maintaining momentum. We have so much growing to do, and people do get impatient and frustrated and tired until some new understanding or learning breaks through. So often a parish in the midst of growth experiences only the growing *pains*, until someone from outside can point out how the group has been growing and changing and *how that helps the rest of us*. It is terribly important for people and parishes to be encouraged and to *know that they are encouraging*. I had the privilege of returning to New Zealand in 1993, a year after our first visit. On this second trip we visited a group of parishes we had stayed with the year before and also people from other areas. There was a sense of "we haven't much to show" when we began our informal conversation; but as they continued to detail their life together, I had to interrupt and note how much had changed in a short year! The lay leadership and participation, without full-time clergy, was impressive. Laypeople were visiting families as preparation for baptism, while others were helping to prepare people for confirmation. Outreach to the elderly and people with other needs had grown and deepened. But it had all happened so naturally that it was hard for them to recognize their strides without outside clarification and affirmation. Total-ministry development relies on that kind of spirit of honest encouragement.

A part of the maintaining-momentum difficulty resides in the stages of total-ministry development. After an initial resistance to change, we have noted a restless enthusiasm to "get on with it." As that kind of growth begins, people focus on the activities of the parish, and this focus can divert the congregation from the continued study that needs to be part of its life; continuing study helps to keep a perspective not only on who they are, but on *whose* they are, not only on what they do, but why and for whom they are doing it. I like to think of this stage as a kind of adolescent period in ministry development, as congregants who go through fascinations with "my ministry" and "our ministry" grow into a more mature understanding of Christ's ministry with, in, and through them and us. But again, the need for continuing education remains

constant throughout total-ministry development as a life-time commitment. It deepens our central acts of worship and keeps us rooted in
Word and directed to Sacrament, acknowledging the godly inspiration
and coordination that ministry requires.

Difficulty Being Overcome: Clericalism

One further development needs to be noted in the diminishing presence
of clericalism, which heralds its disappearance sometime in God's future.
In this diocese there is a notable absence of competition among clergy;
relationships do not rely on which ordination track one has taken. A
considerable and honest collegiality among the ordained is reflected as
well in the clergy-lay relationships. That clergy collegiality is not a
defense against the real or imagined claims of the laity on the clergy. If
any clericalism does exist, it is more likely to be found among the laity,
some of whom still hold to old visions of priesthood and episcopate.
That lingering attitude is neither difficult nor distressing, just different
from the ways we normally relate to one another in this diocese. Clergy
have become sharers in the ministry of Christ entrusted to all of us, serving their particular functions within our common mission. But the old
claims and "shoulds" still surface to remind us that we are not *there* yet.

Stewardship and Money

While the total-ministry process encourages the stewardship of time and
talent, it has some different history when it comes to giving money or
the stewardship of substance. In this "poor" diocese, where our annual
budget is now in the half-million-dollar range, we have seen an annual
marked increase in financial support for the parishes and hence for the
work of the parishes together as diocese. We have no endowments as a
diocese; we live and work on what we get, and the diocesan council is to
be credited with careful and creative stewardship of our resources; the
work does get done and ministry does grow.

And yet a capital funds campaign directed at ministry development
and mission needs instead of buildings netted a smaller amount than
hoped for. The encouraging news was that those who supported the need

for increased mission were the "ordinary" folks who give regularly anyway: middle- and lower-income households that understand the urgency of mission and the role that ministry development has in mission. As testimony to their sense of stewardship, the full-term payments on that now-concluded drive were in the 96 percent range. People who care are faithful; they hang in there. A similar venture to buy land for outreach into a rapidly growing area received similar response from all over the diocese. In this diocese, where the *sound* of money is all around us and the ring of slot machines immediately greets visitors to the airports, those who are able to give more substantially generally do not. They are approached and they are asked, and some of them are courteous, but most of them do not give generously if at all, though some claim membership in the church. Explanations are hard to come by. Some are no longer active Episcopalians, claiming to have been disappointed by the "new" Prayer Book or the ordination of women, but they have committed nowhere else. Others have dealt with some other personal distraction by transferring anger to the church, a behavior that has little or nothing to do with economic status.

I wonder if we are failing to translate total-ministry concerns into a vocabulary that can speak to those reliant on other and older systems, especially systems of power and control. When one's life and livelihood are geared to those very systems, what must a church look like that aspires to servant ministry without undue hierarchy and its attendant controls and power positions? Is there some kind of "game" to be played that acknowledges a dedication to power and control that is contrary to our understanding of where the Spirit leads us in total ministry? More than once I have been challenged to assert power in a situation where, given our understanding of ministry, it would have been grossly inappropriate. The challenge for us is to find ways to communicate the excitement of this shared and extended ministry, and to reclaim and make attractive that sense of a church instituted for mission rather than an institution of comfortable values, a favorite charity.

We have seen some positive response. A casino president had food delivered daily for several months to an emergency shelter for homeless women and children in the basement of one of our small parishes. Another faithful and regular church member has been supportive of a trial ministry in contemporary Christian music in a part of the diocese. A few other generosities have come our way from those who are more privileged than others, but they are outnumbered by denials and polite refusals and, more often, failure to respond in any way. Our imaginations are still seeking ways to attract support to the need for mission. And of course we are seeking help from qualified people in our national stewardship structure. Here again the initiative and the impetus is coming from gifted laypeople who recognize the need for education and a fresh approach to old questions.

Evangelism and Ecumenism

If total ministry is indeed going to be "total," we need to reach out beyond our own household to help and be helped in living into the kingdom of God. For that reason I find it difficult to separate evangelism from ecumenical sharing. Denominational evangelism often resolves into church-growth patterns, which is a timely direction in which to travel. But the Good News as embodied in Jesus has a wider range, notably in the Johannine passages about "one flock, one shepherd," and the high priestly prayer in John 17 and its petition for unity. The proclamation of the Good News is meant to be shared beyond theological and administrative boundaries as witness to the central hope-fact that we are one in Christ.

Judicatory conversations are most certainly steps in the right direction for healing our divisions. But the real energy comes from the grass roots, where we work together in living out the Good News, especially in the areas of social ministry. Our experience has been that our minority (in this area) denomination can initiate a program for the poor or the hungry or the homeless or those in prison or all of the above and help comes from many directions. The aforementioned homeless shelter for women and children started out in an Episcopal church basement, and immediate help came from some Roman Catholic Franciscans. Now in its own building, the shelter has workers and supporters from a wide variety of faith expressions. Another effort to help mainstream the homeless began with a deacon's vision and now has a board that includes civic representatives, other denominations, and a Muslim leader. And so it goes: the planting of seeds, the shared watering and nurturing. The Good News is being lived out among the poor, which certainly has a solid biblical base!

In another vein, the former warden of one of our parishes has great expertise in a form of martial arts. He has begun and developed a class for that, using its discipline as an attraction for local youth of any or no religious persuasion. Each session is framed in a form of prayer and continues with the development of respect for oneself and for others— sound familiar? Commandment becomes discipline and lifestyle. Out of this program has come Saint Luke's karate team, which travels and wins awards. The team is the first imaginative, programmatic step toward a "center for community" to be built on the church grounds to serve just as its name explains. Total-ministry development is by definition and by biblical example inclusive. We do not lose our identity or sacrifice our traditions by sharing ministry in these ways, nor do we ask others to lose theirs. But we are careful not to hallow those traditions more than our common Lord, who continues to lead his church into new adventures and deeper commitments to the good news of God's kingdom and reign.

Isn't that the true root for honest evangelism? For evangelism is willing to acknowledge that the Lord is still in charge and that the Lord still speaks to the contemporary generation with good news. Total-ministry development allows people to be centered in the Good News in a way that speaks clearly to the other forces at work in a local community. It is more transformation-by-example than battery-by-Bible as God's word gets lived out visibly and intelligently. When people accept the momentum of their baptismal covenant and the essential community in which they are included and embraced, evangelism happens—as a way of living more than as a program for church growth; yet, oddly, growth is what happens as a result!

Youth

If we are to be honest about total-ministry development, we need to include all ages. For too long we have told our children selected Bible stories as models for behavior. At the same time we ask them, "What are you going to be when you grow up?" That question bears the distinct message that "you aren't much now." We have been slow in addressing this important area of ministry development, but a recent diocesan convention put us on a new course: "Youth work" begins in preschool and continues through grade 12; it is essentially giving children and youth work to do, acknowledging that they are ministers for Christ *and* giving them the freedom to help define the work of ministry with the rest of us. In turn, including younger people allows the older generations to grow with them.

We are in the process of developing a comprehensive program that will function in addition to church-school classes. In this program children will have the opportunity to minister to others in age-appropriate ways, building on activities that have been around for some time. Possibilities include kindergartners making cards for children who are ill or convalescing. The intent is to allow the children to value their part in the ministry that includes us all and to make a continuing connection to their own baptism. We hope to deliver their contributions from being "cute" to being valued as ministry.

Some people are working on a greater involvement of children of all ages in the liturgy. Others are developing age-appropriate areas of ministry in the community, while still others are exploring how we train disciples and send them into the ordinary places of their lives—school, playground, team sports, and so on—without setting them up for peer rejection and irrelevance. We want to encourage example-as-witness rather than a religious exhibitionism. In these developments some of our older youth (junior and senior high) have taken creative leadership roles, and we are listening carefully to their counsel.

Instead of wringing our hands over "where have the young people gone?" we are repenting of having left them out of the church's ministry. We see our children and youth as co-workers with us in the total-ministry adventure in which the Spirit leads us.

Summary

I see us being led into a dimension of faith that will allow the church to take itself less seriously than it takes our Lord. So much of our time has been spent on ecclesiastical introspection and consequent infighting and on building up an institution or diagnosing its illnesses and bemoaning its decline. Our adventure in total ministry gives strong indications that, once we begin to accept Christ's ministry among us and stretching us beyond ourselves, we become a different church: a working organism more than a religious organization. As that kind of ministry development continues, we expect significant changes. The way we gather to do "the business of God" has already changed significantly and is perceived as good news. We are already seeing changes in how we fund what we fund, due to some enthusiasms and some resistances at either end of the scale. We are struggling to redefine what is important for us as church, sadly relinquishing some of the old ways to work through the discomfort of new challenges and new priorities. The first great commandment assumes a new power as we focus on who is central and who is really in charge or in control of this organism's life. The second commandment about loving one's neighbor becomes all the more urgent as we surrender, however reluctantly, old self-satisfactions, prejudices, and unholy opinions.

One of the most interesting and helpful developments to date has been the gradual release from a kind of congregationalism that has long been a part of the Episcopal Church's unwritten tradition and which had nurtured a kind of adversarial stance of local parish to diocese: "us" and "them." It still surfaces now and then, but now it is a surprise rather than a given. The old categorical systems and the structures that grew out of them were far more conducive to that particular kind of insular congregationalism. Total-ministry development moves people and parishes into relationships that extend beyond the local scene. In Nevada this means that *diocese* is becoming the primary unit for the Episcopal Church.

Perhaps coincidence—or a bit of prophetic insight—led two friends in a former parish to give me the same plaque for my office wall, which I have noted earlier in another context. It is a picture of a sailing ship with this message: "A ship is safe in a harbor, but that's not what ships are for." A vision for total ministry sees this *nave*, this church, as called out to the dangers and opportunities of the high seas—or the desert or the mountains or the plains beyond—with all its members as active crew, bearing the "cargo" of good news where the wind or the Spirit will direct them.

So as we speak of continuing developments in this context, we reflect a dimension of responsible faith that enables us to follow without mutiny, without seizing control. It is a dimension of faith that we recognize as humility: an openness to the One who knows where we need to go and with whom we need to travel. That does not involve a lack of responsibility or a failure to plan. There is no human organization that can match the miracle of the human organism. It is, once again, simply a question of where the center is, where the worth-ship is.

CHAPTER 7

Looking Ahead

Humility can be dangerous. Being open to the Spirit can become dangerous living. For the wind *does* blow where it will. It can be received as a
source of energy, but it cannot be controlled. Its speed and direction can
be measured in some ways, and that is what we try to do as we continue
our exploration of total ministry. So you might say we are scanning the
horizon to see where this "desert ship" is being blown or directed.

Ordained Ministry and Ordination Rites

One of the most critical areas still remains in the ordained ministry and
the kinds of hierarchy it represents. Some of that is encouraged in our
ordination rites, and I would encourage those in other denominations to
revisit their own ordination rites with that sensitivity. I repeat one and
offer a few other examples of ways our ordination rites bespeak hierarchy.

How We Pray

A post-Communion prayer in the ordination rites for deacon, priest, and
bishop undermines the sense of equality in ministry within the body, as it
speaks of "raising up" the person who has just been admitted to "holy"
orders. ("We thank you for raising up among us faithful servants for the
ministry of your Word and Sacraments.") "Raising up" is the kind of
vertical vocabulary that cannot escape the hierarchical implications many

in the church have enjoyed and will defend as necessary to a well-defined (clerically centered) structure. Others might observe with us that such vocabulary is the beginning of the temptations to presumption. An alternative for us is the use of a post-Communion prayer from the eucharistic liturgy, where we ask that God will "send *us* out to do the work you have given *us* to do." That is a better fit with our understanding of total ministry.

I remember the first ordination at which I presided. Interpolated in the service of ordination to the priesthood was an owning and affirmation of ministry by the entire congregation. The parish wardens asked for those who expressed ministry in a number of church and community areas to stand, until all but one or two visitors (who were a bit confused by this process) were standing; in that context I laid my hands on the ordinand, aware of an entire ministering community very visible among the invisibly attendant angels, archangels, and all the company of heaven. Instead of being nervous about "doing it right" the first time, I found myself moved into a whole new understanding of what I was doing as a part of the ministering community on whose behalf I was acting. It was a servant action, and it felt and feels right. That has become a standard part of our local clergy ordinations, and we continue to educate congregations to own their expressions of ministry in this visible way so that they can tell others about it and include others in this basic understanding.

A Different Temper

That is not always so with the ordination of seminary graduates, for they often bring an entirely different and outside community to celebrate this milestone. In some ways, such ordinations have a sense of "wedding" to them—not marriage, but wedding—with special people brought in to do special things before they disperse once again; in that there is a kind of *setting up*, if not raising up. I traveled recently to another diocese to ordain a transitional deacon from and of Nevada to the priesthood. She was engaged in a program of full-time nonparochial work, but she had identified with and been embraced by a congregation in the community where she and her husband were living. It was a fine occasion with special people participating; afterwards she wrote to observe that the congregation now was treating her differently "now that you're really ordained," as if her ministry prior to that did not count as such or as much! Having met and enjoyed members of that congregation, I know their intent is one of affirmation and inclusion, but there are still those intimations of hierarchy sneaking in from the corners of our history.

We look ahead to a time when such nods to hierarchy can be replaced by that sense of participation in the worshipping and ministering community that we now experience in the ordination of local clergy. That kind of development will depend on a radical change in how seminaries and dioceses relate, and how dioceses and bishops, or any other judicatory leaders with responsibility for seminarians, understand their roles in the formation of clergy who are set within the community rather than "raised up" over it.

In the process that leads to the ordination of local clergy, training and formation are done within the calling community. As the ministry of every baptized person is affirmed in that formation process, there is no need to elevate those on an ordination track to higher level of ministry. When one is sent off to seminary, however, there is the assumption that one will be formed for priesthood there, usually according to cultural and geographical norms that have more history than contemporary relevance.

Keeping the Pastoral Connection

There is something to be learned or really to be *re*-learned by returning to the importance of a calling or commending community. In the case of seminarians sent off to a seminary, there is the urgent need for more personal support by the local congregation and the judicatory leadership. Formation can continue to occur in that local context, as the seminarian is encouraged to return and retreat with members of the congregation and to rely on the bishop or other judicatory leader for some measure of spiritual direction. The center then moves from getting ready for ordination to the temper of a shared spiritual journey of which ordination may be a part.

My own experience in this area has been instructive, though I need to note that this diocese does not send large numbers of people off to seminary. When candidates do go away, I ask that they go to a seminary within my travel range, so that I may visit with them on a more frequent and regular basis than I could if they were across the country. This arrangement does not provide an intensive space of spiritual direction, but it does allow for a relationship wherein we know each other and can share insights and difficulties about the seminary experience. The most basic difficulty lies in the very varied expectations of different judicatories. Some still send students to be "formed" at and by the seminary. That creates a climate where alternative means toward and definitions of that goal are easily caught up in the tensions and anxieties of the other claims regarding formation. Redefining what *formation* means in the context of a growing commitment to total-ministry development requires some urgent and honest conversations among judicatory leaders and seminary deans and faculties.

Different denominations have their own versions of or aversions to hierarchical structures. It is not my intent to deal with those in this context, except to encourage once again a close look at "ministerial formation" with that sensitivity to the ministry of all the baptized and the place of the ordained person in the community's midst. It is interesting to note that, in some of the newer denominations, formed in the past decade or two, there is a very strong emphasis on clerical hierarchy and authority, which throws our own experience of that into bold relief.

More about Rites

In the ordination rites of the Episcopal Church, both those being ordained deacon and priest are asked if they will "obey your bishop and other ministers who may have authority *over* you and your work" (italics mine). That becomes all the more significant when we find no such question in the ordination of a bishop, that the bishop be accountable to other ministers, indeed the body whom that person is called to serve.

There is no need to pick apart the ordination rites in great detail here, but we feel the strong and urgent need for ways of expressing a nonhierarchical ministering community as we define tasks needed to strengthen that community and set people within the community to perform them. We look for and even offer some leadership in developing ordination rites that might not, to quote the Prayer Book, "give your Holy Spirit" to special people for holy work, but rather acknowledge the holy work of all the baptized who are *all* given the Holy Spirit and led by that same Spirit to inspired, committed, and effective service.

Given the number of ecumenical conversations in process, it would
be exciting to do this kind of exploration across denominational lines and
live more closely into the vision of that unity for which we all pray. In
such a cooperative process, we would have the opportunity to explore the
varied understandings of power and authority in each tradition and to
balance them against the rich strains of servanthood and centeredness
found in each tradition. Since ordination rites are really occasions for
worship and thus central to our understanding of who we are and whose
we are, it seems essential to look at such serious revisions that will center
the whole worshipping community rather than raise up a few among
them.

Local Bishops

While I understand that only the Episcopal and Roman Catholic churches
require the presence of a bishop for the laying on of hands or for confirmation, I believe that most so-called "major" denominations do require
some form of judicatory presence at ordinations. In many populous or
geographically extensive areas, that can mean considerable travel and,
for some leaders, the sense of being a confirming or ordaining "ma-
chine."

While that is not a pressing problem in this diocese, it does lead us
to wonder about the possibilities and benefits of allowing for a judicatory
presence in smaller areas, to help provide the close pastoral relationship
so key to a healthy and growing church. We see the office of episcopacy
heading toward a more clearly defined servanthood role, carefully integrated into the gifted body as a kind of leaven to foster growth and depth.

We have already noted the Episcopal Church canon providing for
the calling, training, and ordination of local deacons and priests. It is
within the realm of possibility that the canon providing for local clergy
be expanded to allow for the calling of "local bishops." It would be
important to be very clear that, unlike some other local judicatory pre-
sences, the local bishop would have only a pastoral function and not an
administrative one.

We wonder about using the same process of call, deeply rooted in
study and prayer, to call local bishops in critical areas of a jurisdiction.
Their function would not be unlike the role of our regional vicars as

extended episcopate, but their presence as employed or retired people in the area with the added dimension of close episcopal availability might well refocus the judicatory role. In this area, we have much to learn from some of the more Protestant denominations.

Changing a Vision

The problem of "who's *really* in charge?" or "where does the buck stop?" needs to be restated—or embodied in a different sense of relationships within the episcopate or judicatory leadership. For in restating the questions of accountability and authority, we come to a point of real sacrifice and reformation. In place of the buck-stopping role (which is really focused on problems), the bishops in a given jurisdiction will discover a relationship grounded in service and energized by a vision of the church at work. It is a vision that sees the leadership role as servant to a community vision (rather than a merely episcopal or judicatorial one), with the extended episcopal role as one of encouragement to growth in mission. Problems arise in the life of any religious community, to be sure, but they are better not "solved" by a person in a hierarchical relationship to the community; far better to have a fairly local presence to encourage community response to and responsibility for the problems they face and the possibilities that beckon them.

As a significant aside, we do need to note that the current focus for many denominations is problem oriented or "issue driven." Much of that revolves around a change in religious understanding and expression and the ways in which people react to such changes. It is more than unfortunate that often people respond to change by quarrelling over whom to exclude from the life and/or leadership of the organization. Such argument results in people going off in a huff to their own backyards. Or, even more seriously, it transforms the center of the church's vocation into a nest of problems rather than a beacon of hope and commitment to mission. We seem to get all tied up in the wrong issues.

In that kind of climate, the expectation for leadership is to arbitrate or "decide" rather than to mediate using the gifts of listening, prayer, and holy conversation. How much more effective it would be not to have the bishop rush in as a "trouble shooter," focused only on the problem, but to move beyond that to the real needs beneath the surface. I am reminded here of my "white charger syndrome" to which I confessed in an earlier chapter and from which the vicars have helped me repent. What a difference it would make to have a local bishop in the community or region be present as a "thanksgiver" who can provide a continuing immediacy in that part of the body—someone who was not elected in a highly charged process but called in the reliance on the Holy Spirit: a bishop who is not a paid administrator, but one who works alongside others on common ground.

There is still room and need for a diocesan bishop, especially given some of the canonical requirements for bishops. Other denominations may experience the same need for some kind of structural centering. Beyond the canons there is the additional ministry of reaching out beyond one's boundaries to consult and commune with and learn from the experiences and adventures of other dioceses and other denominations. And there is still the important role, properly assigned to a denominational leader, to be custodian of the shared vision of the church in a specific locale.

Many problems will present themselves in this kind of reformation. Aren't problems the required meat and drink of judicatory leaders? That becomes the first sacrifice: to refocus on the call to mission and *whose mission it is*. In that process, structure is not abolished or torn down, but it is refashioned to accommodate mission rather than institutional organization. To use the image of an office building, the vision is for a structure without elevators. There are open doors between the rooms on one level, where the flow of traffic is internal only in so far as it points to the outside through main doors that open both ways. There are plenty of "exit" signs that point the church out to the fields of service and of harvest.

This is the kind of adventure into which total ministry leads us, and it bespeaks a vision of hope rather than a commitment to problems. If that sounds even slightly utopian, the vision is skewed; for painful sacrifice of long-held customs is very much a part of such reformation, and the acceptance of a well-centered truth instead of a need to control may be the most difficult change we have to face.

That is the spirit behind the development of a "local" episcopate. The mechanics of how to get there will continue to challenge us and invite us into uncharted territories and even significant reformation and sacrifice.

Forever and . . . ?

One of the touchiest issues in the context of ordained ministry lies in the sense of the indelibility of orders: "Once a priest, always a priest." That is not a strain that runs through all denominations, but it is significant enough to address in this context, for the notion of indelibility serves the very kind of hierarchy that we offer for transformation.

Indelibility suggests a direct relationship between God and the ordained person in which the community is not involved save as a recipient of the ordained person's gifts. There is some Old Testament precedent for such a vocation. I believe that is mitigated in the New Testament example of Jesus, yet given some endorsement in the apostleship of Paul. Paul himself, however, is the one who gives great weight to the one Spirit who coordinates the whole body for equal and interdependent service. The question that arises most certainly in the context of total ministry development is this: Where is the identity of the ordained person without a community from which that person is called and in which that person serves? If we are to hold to the vision that God calls leaders, must they be ordained people or can they be others who gather for God in the wider community?

Part of the total-ministry picture is that a person's license to officiate as an ordained person ends when her or his relationship to the calling community ends. This provision applies only to those locally called and ordained under Title III, Canon 9, which stipulates that they are called to serve in one place. (See the canonical text in the appendix. See also the Diocese of Nevada agreement statement, in endnote 1, chapter 2.) Yet even when a local clergyperson moves from the calling parish, there is still a claim that the person in question is still a priest, though no longer licensed to officiate.

Perhaps the more serious question about indelibility comes in the baptismal context. Baptism is an indelible sacrament. And it is holy baptism that ordains a Christian for ministry; to be a Christian is to be a minister. Is that not enough? Is there some reason why some of us need another indelible identity, to improve on that given in baptism? Or is indelibility just another expression of hierarchy, of somehow being "better"? We have no ready answer to such questions, nor is there any desire to discredit ordained ministry. It is important to put ordained ministry into an honest context that does not contradict the sense of

Christian vocation given in baptism and that remains faithful to an ec-
clesiology that celebrates God as center and us as interdependent, Spirit-
filled servants. In this concern about the claimed indelibility of the ordained, we come up against the same hierarchical issues we have seen in
other areas; as always the question is whether or not such hierarchical
concepts are helpful and whether they serve to foster or distract the call
to mission issued to all the baptized.

Reclaiming an Old Word

Mission is a vocation extended by God to a servant church, which in
God's mercy is guided and coordinated by the Holy Spirit. Given that
understanding, I would like to call this diocese a *charismatic* diocese,
focusing not on particular gifts and their use or abuse, but upon the
Giver, who takes our varying, wonderful, common, mundane, and even
weird gifts and fashions out of them a functioning organism that embodies good news in a local and global context. In such an organism, as Paul
notes in 1 Corinthians 12, there is an essential equality based on interdependence or co-ordination, and we understand that to be expressed in
baptism. So there are no "better" or "higher" gifts, though there may be
claims to the contrary. That is simply another sign of sin, which sepa-
rates gifts from gifts, one person from another, people from God. If the
body that Paul describes is to have any integrity, it must own that interdependence and equality of persons, indeed respecting the dignity of
every human being, a promise we offer in baptismal covenant.
    Such a renewed vision of the church *as we can see it in our own
local expressions* cuts through turf issues, which are often the most serious battlegrounds in church life. There is even a sense of "theological
turf," where one group may claim to have a far greater apprehension of
the truth than others. Allowing the Spirit to have control and listening
for that direction preempts the need for "my" or "our" turf. Turf prompts
a defensive attitude and stance, another way of dividing and separating,
whereas we are called into a unity of the Spirit in the bond of peace.
Another way of expressing the coordinative function of the Spirit is to
note that coordination puts the members of the body into relationship
because interdependence is an expression of relationship. Interdependence incarnates the body-members' relationship in Christ, expressed as

truth and truth-bearing. It is also instructive to note that, in the biblical witness, the Spirit sometimes transports people from one place to another place altogether!

An organism that can allow preeminence to the Giver of the gifts is truly charismatic no matter what its worship style; I am persuaded that if total-ministry development is not overorganized or systematized beyond recognition, it will lead us into being a people gifted by God for the mission of bearing and being good news as a charismatic, gifted, Spirit-filled community.

The Scope of the Mission

In these pages mission may often seem primarily a local witness. There is a reason for this. In our experience, when people in parishes can understand the possibilities for mission—the needs, the pains, the joys—in their own environments, they are far more likely to respond to the same in a wider context. One small parish in a former mining town has a real sense of its place and its witness in its own community, and they bring that understanding to their support of a missionary in South America and in response to the ministry of the Presiding Bishop's Fund for World Relief. And there are others with the same understanding and perspective. This local-to-global sense of mission may be hard to understand as it can lead to an evasive temptation, as noted before in these pages: "Once we have our own house in order, then we'll be ready for outreach." That definition of *outreach* may be directed to no more than getting more members, so that our house can be in even better order. Or it may show itself in small financial contributions to worthy causes in the community without personal involvement.

Total ministry leads to the *embodiment* of mission, and that is a necessarily local option. Total ministry accepts the momentum of baptism and the baptismal covenant, which combines the will to express the Good News with the reliance on Christ the center, the Giver of gifts for ministry and for life itself: "I will with God's help." And that momentum cannot be contained. It spreads.

How does that work? One woman keeps her car trunk full of various sizes of clothing and shoes, ready to help when asked by a homeless person on the street; she regularly relays to the parish specific needs of the community at Sunday worship. Another man tries to include this kind of mission entry in his conversation once a week: "That's interesting, but our church has a different way of coming at that." Still others show up at prison every Wednesday night to listen to and pray with prisoners. Others lobby the city councils or state offices on behalf of services for the poor. One disabled person spends hours on the phone each week, talking with those who are shut in also and offering a ministry of prayer. Some preach the gospel simply by *being there* in their daily business, even daring to challenge destructive or other hurtful behaviors. One woman tells of confronting a co-worker kindly about her frequent use of abusive language, with the result that months later that co–worker came and asked where and how to go to church, for she had felt the attraction of kindness instead of superior religious judgment.

Total ministry affirms that where you are counts, that where you are is the mission field. It affirms that the mission is centered in the good news of Jesus Christ, and that it bears the embrace of acceptance rather than the test of Being Right. Mission outreach attracts people into a shared relationship with Jesus Christ, from which truth emerges and is experienced. The spirit of total ministry, then, creates a mentality and a spirituality of encouragement, with its attendant image of embrace and its holy theme of acceptance as essential in mission.

Total-ministry development also moves people into community, so that their spiritual experience is not confined to individual and lonely celebration. The baptismal vocation is to be together as church, to be one in Christ, to be participants in a many-peopled story. As people grow in their parish's exploration of total ministry, they are always accountable to the community: How are *we* approaching this local need? Where are we being—or failing to be—good news? Where does my gift fit, or are there other gifts I may not be acknowledging? The list of questions could continue, on and on, addressing the need to express community beyond individuality while still honoring individuality as contributor to community.

A Wider Context

That same spirit moves local mission into a wider context. It may begin by crossing borders: going to another parish in another diocese to share with other curious searchers the experience of total ministry. Several of our clergy and laity have made such visits. One small parish on the "east coast" of Nevada went to another remote diocese to share the possibilities in being a tiny church; it was an especially affirming event. One priest and her husband, a preacher-in-training, spent a weekend at a two-denomination parish in a neighboring diocese, presenting a message of their parish community's journey as a story of total-ministry development. Laity and clergy have visited the church in Aotearoa, New Zealand and Polynesia, and we have welcomed to Nevada laity and clergy from there, as well as from Canada, Africa, and England, jointly exploring how total ministry can be developed and how the Spirit really can be trusted with more than local "models." In these developing relationships, one is not teaching and the other receiving. We explore together, making no claims on how ministry development may be expressed in different climates and contexts. We look forward to an increase in such nondefensive and unpretentious conversation. And we do so with this essential awareness: We move into mission where we are so that we can have a vision of the larger world in which God's people live and serve in communion with us. We continue to learn the truth that total ministry is organic more than it is programmatic.

Again, we are not dealing with a model-based system for which a bishop or a diocese can claim authorship and hence exercise some real or imagined control. We are dealing with the generosity of the Spirit, who is moving gracefully in the seeking church. And it is there that we find the courage to listen—to the Spirit and to others on the same or parallel tracks for ways of living into and expressing the mission to which we have been called as baptized Christians. We look ahead to the time when that vision can be central to the ministry of all the baptized.

The Growing Edge

Some years ago I was on a silent retreat with a group of priests who were part of an extended continuing education program. Early in that quiet time, one of the retreat leaders asked me, "Where is your growing edge?"

I gave several immediate, facile, and most unsatisfactory answers focused on "what I would/should do" without reference to the community of which I was a part; my considerations were based mainly on "what I know about myself now" instead of where I needed to follow and be led.

God does provide antidotes to such spiritual poison. I returned to my single room following that conference with the retreat leader. I had set everything out on the small wooden desk: Prayer Book, Bible, and my own journal, the tools I would use to achieve some measure of individual holiness during the retreat. I casually glanced into the desk drawer and noticed there a pile of papers, apparently left by some other occupant of the room. I closed the drawer, not wishing to intrude on another's privacy. But on impulse I reopened the drawer (the Spirit made me do it!) and began to read those papers. They were notes from a number of people who had inhabited that same room at various times, and they gave testimony to how their lives had been enriched, threatened, changed as they gave themselves to prayer. They became harder to read as I was moved to tears—and to repentance. I knew that I was part of a community, some of whom I could not see, and that retreat ceased to be a time of individual improvement; it became a time of recentering in community. The unseen community moved me with fresh vision into the community I could see and with whom I share a special joy.

That same tension exists as a church takes on a vision for total ministry. Total-ministry development does not involve simply reorganizing the way we do things now or "making me better." It leads us into fresh adventure where we are not in complete control. The growing edge is just that: It is on the outskirts of our experience, as the Spirit calls us to trust and venture further. Of course resistance is a part of that journey because the call is from comfort into risk, but it is a risk that includes enjoyment. I do wish we could learn to distinguish between comfort and enjoyment. The joy of the Gospel transcends the ease of living and managing. Total-ministry development seeks to express the joy in discipleship.

I noted earlier how community people living near some of our smaller churches have noticed a new spirit of fun emanating from the congregation as its members share the responsibilities of ministry; some people who had lapsed over some timely issue or personal disagreement felt the tug to return to the church just to find out what was happening! Ministers of the Good News embody the joy inherent in our faith. Without that sense of joy in Christ, our mission can convey little but desperate sympathy to the world where God sends and plants us. Joy in Christ recognizes personal and social healing as achievable. And that joy finds its strength in company—community, communion, shared ministry—in ways that none of us can find alone.

So we get a new sense of mission imperative as people study and pray together, as they ask questions not only about their parish's internal coordination, but also about where they go from here where they fit out there. In some of our parishes, that has already had significant effect, which in turn is celebrated by the whole diocese. (We emphasize cele-bration much more than trouble shooting.) Other parishes are listening to their neighbors and asking questions and sharing insights as they develop a mission strategy in which we can all share.

Sin does happen—if not abound—in such a climate, as individuals or groups cling to old models or simply enjoy complaining about change. In my years in this diocese, however, I have seen that kind of resistance diminish considerably, as the Spirit generates a new kind of enthusiasm and acceptance of a growing edge.

That growing edge has led us into some mistakes that have been educational. At times the vicars and I have been hasty in making or implementing changes without sharing them with the larger body in the diocese. I remember being taken to account for a new way of affirming local vocations. We had discovered a very gifted person who could serve best as a priest to some very marginal communities, and I asked the parish of which he was a part to affirm this diocesan call to ordained service. They refused, not because of any difficulties with the person, but because we had not taken the time to share the vision of what we were trying to do and how it affected our common mission in the dio-cese. I needed to go and visit with the vestry and offer explanation, with which they agreed. They also offered an admonition to avoid assumption and share the vision!

Our enthusiasm for moving onto the growing edge has allowed some people to feel adrift without oars or sails for a time, which in turn has been greater cause for celebration when "land" was sighted and found. Our enthusiasm has led some others to try a simple reorganization of their life together, which eventually has proved to be unsatisfying and ineffective. Our enthusiasm has also allowed us to realize that the real test is not how well we function as an institution, but how much we touch others in the name and spirit of Jesus Christ.

Several years ago in New Zealand, I had the opportunity to meet with the small and delightful House of Bishops for Aotearoa, New Zealand, and Polynesia. We were all together in one place for a partners-in-mission consultation. During our conversation, one of the bishops asked me to articulate my vision for the Diocese of Nevada. While I had to acknowledge that my vision was not necessarily central to our progress, I did confess, much to my own surprise and some of theirs, that I hoped the Diocese of Nevada could become a well-disorganized diocese.

That was not a vote for chaos, though chaos is the context for creation when God is in control. I do see us on the road away from institutional self-preoccupation, though not away from necessary structures. I do not see our mission as having to change or reshape all the structures of the church. That is an institutional navel-gazing that distracts us from our commission. We spend too much time evaluating and in some instances justifying our own structures, rather than using them to bear fruit. I see us as continuing a process already begun in moving away from old models and systems to a point where these conditions prevail: (1) a reliance on God the Holy Spirit to provide the healthy center in which we are refreshed and strengthened and from which we grow, rooted; (2) a sense of being a well-ordered organism mindful of our need for community in order to act as community; (3) a theology of relationship that knows truth as being in Christ ("the grace of our Lord Jesus Christ") and embodies that in mission; and (4) a keen awareness that we are about the Good News that transforms the world.

So as diocese or church in this place, we maintain a communion of concern and encouragement, accepting the realities of the stuff (sin) that works against the expressions of goodness in life and accepting the realities of blessing and growth in life. As a diocese we come together to celebrate our center and to listen, learn, and share how we continue to respond to the Lord's commission to "be" and to "go." And that is our growing edge, to be an organic rather than only programmatic church—exhibiting patience and trust, for it does not happen in just a few days or months or even years. Wes Frensdorff noted that it would take several generations for such changes to take root.

It is particularly appropriate to note that church size and "success" are of less concern than momentum and faithfulness. For spiritual faithfulness and momentum overcome the fear of chaos that often accompanies such exploration and imagination. In the understanding of truth as resident in our relationship to Jesus Christ, there is the freedom to be

who we are, as we are, where we are, and as we are growing to be mis-
sioners in Christ, ambassadors for Christ.

What's New?

In our experience of total-ministry development, the answer to the "what's
new?" question would be "very little." Innovation is not a primary virtue
in the kinds of changes brought by total-ministry development. Indeed,
to picture ourselves as innovators would be to succumb to the temptations that quickly shift the center of ministry from where it belongs to
our own genius and/or cleverness. It is important to recall the ending to
Luke's account of Jesus' temptations in the wilderness: "When the devil
had finished every test, he departed from him until an opportune time"
(Luke 4:13). In the context of ministry development, such opportune
times are frequent. We are tempted to see ourselves as the creators rather
than as the recipients of gifts, to forget that we are those whose sight has
been restored to see and follow the Lord who touches us.
    We are not innovators. And yet "very little is new" is not a way of
saying that we have gone back to the mythical purity of the early church.
To be sure, we struggle with the same issues of control and division that
have marked the church's experience in every age, but there is really no
going back. In the place of needing to do anything "new" or "old," we
find instead a kind of refreshment that comes from listening together in
community. There are no "stars," ordained or lay. The bishop is not
leading the diocese into greater health and better managed systems.
There is a sense of shared adventure, together with some shared resistance. There is a growing commitment to sharing vision more readily
without fear of putdowns or other power responses. And there is a strong
spirit of repentance, in the sense of being open to the changes to which
God calls us; we dare to live with the holy stress that such a response to
change places on old systems and firm opinions. Repentance and conversion are the true doors into the kinds of systemic change toward
which total-ministry development steers. Underlying all this is a basic
respect for those with whom we work and worship, recognizing that it is
the Spirit at work among us.
    Above all, while we acknowledge the importance and benefit of
well-planned and focused programs for ministry development and

experiments that may seem "far out" at times, we know that looking ahead means looking to the center of our faith; for unless ministry development is primarily a spiritual journey, it is a wheel spinning at great cost to those whom we are called to serve.

We look ahead to the fruits of a repentance and conversion that will allow the Gospel to be embodied in all ministers for God. So the "future" vision is consistent with the beginning: "The time is fulfilled, and the kingdom of God has come near; repent and believe in the good news" (Mark 1:15).

And that is where we become the search lights to find and even to be identified with the angels who reveal God's presence in the world.

Canons Regarding Ordination of Local Clergy

In 1970, Title III, Canon 8 read as follows:

Of Admission to Holy Orders in Special Cases

Sec. 1. In special cases, the requirements of the Normal Standard of Learning may be modified as hereinafter provided. But, in every case, before a Deacon shall be ordered Priest, he shall be examined, by the Bishop and two Presbyters, in the office and work of a Priest and as to his ability to serve the Church in that Order of Ministry.

Sec. 2.(a). With regard to communities which are small, isolated, remote, or distinct in respect of ethnic composition, language, or culture, and which can be supplied only intermittently with the sacramental and pastoral ministrations of the Church, it shall be competent for the Bishop, with the advice and consent of the Standing Committee or Council of Advice, and with the prior approval in principle of the House of Bishops of the Province, to seek out and ordain to the Diaconate, and not less than six months later to the Priesthood, a resident of the said community, after a period of Candidacy (pursuant to Canon III.2, Section 5(d) of not less than six-months' duration).

(b). The person to be ordained under the provisions of this Section shall have the following qualifications:

(1). He shall be not less than thirty-two years of

age, and shall have been a member of this Church
in good standing for at least five years.

(2). He shall have been a regular attendant upon
the stated services of the Church, and faithful in
resorting to the Sacraments when available, and
a regular contributor of record to the support of
the Church.

(3). He shall be reputed in the community to
have comported himself as a Christian in his
personal and family life and in his dealings with
others in the community.

(4). He shall satisfy the Bishop and the Committee on Ministry of the Diocese of District of
his ability to read the Holy Scriptures and conduct the services of the Church in an intelligible,
seemly, and reverent fashion.

(c). If a Deacon or Priest who has been ordained in accordance
with this Canon shall subsequently remove to another community within the Diocese or District, he shall be entitled to exercise his ministry in that place only if he be licensed thereto by
the Bishop. Such Ministers shall not be granted Letters Dimissory to another Diocese or District without the request, in
writing, of the Bishop of the Diocese or District to which he
wishes to remove.

Sec. 3. In all cases of the ordination under this Canon of men
with modified requirements of learning, a record of the modifications shall be kept by the Bishop, and the standing of every
Minister thus ordained shall be reported to the Recorder with the
other matters required in Canon I.1, Sec. 4(b).

By 1991, it had been renumbered Canon 9 and reads as follows:

Of the Ordination of Local Priests and Deacons

Sec. 1.(a). With regard to Dioceses with Congregations or missionary opportunities in communities which are small, isolated, remote, or distinct in respect to ethnic composition, language, or culture, and which cannot be provided sufficiently with the sacraments and pastoral ministrations of the Church through Clergy ordained under the provision of Canon III.7, it shall be permissible for the Bishop, with the advice and consent of the Standing Committee, or the equivalent body in special jurisdictions, and with the prior approval in principle of the House of Bishops of the Province, to establish procedures by which persons may be called by their Congregations and the Bishop with the Standing Committee, to be ordained local Priests and Deacons and licensed to serve the Congregations or communities out of which they were called.

(b). The persons to be ordained under the provisions of this Section shall have the following qualifications:

> (1). They shall be not less than thirty-two years of age, and shall have been members of this Church for at least five years. Under extraordinary circumstances, the Bishop and the Standing Committee, on a two-thirds vote, may allow a variance of either of these qualifications, but in no case below the ages specified in Canons III.6 and III.7.

> (2). They shall be confirmed adult communicants in good standing, recognized by their Congregation for their maturity in Christian Faith and Life.

> (3). They shall be recognized as leaders in the Congregation and shall be firmly rooted in the community.

(4). If no suitable person be found within the local Congregation, the Bishop and the Congregation with the consent of a two-thirds of the Standing Committee may call a person who resides in another community of the Diocese but otherwise satisfies all the requirements of this Canon.

Sec. 2. The provisions for Postulancy and Candidacy, as set forth in Canon III.4.2(c) through 8 and Canon III.5.1 through 5, tshall be followed, except that:

(a). The certificate required in Canon III.4.4(d)(2) shall be signed by:

> (1). Four confirmed adult communicants in good standing from the Congregation resident in the community, if there is no local council of the Congregation; and

> (2). One Presbyter of the Diocese to whom the applicant and the community are personally known, if there is no Member of the Clergy in charge of the Congregation.

(b). No minimum time for study as a Postulant shall apply in Canon III.5.1(b).

(c). Letters Dimissory shall not be required.

Sec. 3. For those who are to serve their Congregations as lo-Priests, the provision as set forth in Canon III.7 shall be followed, except that:

(a). The requirements of the standards of learning specified in Canon III.7.5 may be modified, but in every case:

> (1). The Bishop and the Commission must re-reive satisfactory evidence that the Candidate:

(i). Understands the office and
work of a Deacon and of a
Priest and is ready to serve in
that Order to which the Candidate is called;

(ii). Has adequate knowledge of
the contents of the Old and New
Testaments, Church History and
of the Church's teaching as set
forth in the Creeds and in An
Outline of the Faith, commonly
called the Catechism; and

(iii). Is familiar with the Book
of Common Prayer and has the
ability to read the Holy Scriptures and conduct the service of
the Church in an intelligible and
reverent fashion.

(2). The Bishop and Commission shall require
and supervise the continuing education of each
person ordained under the provisions of this
Canon, and keep a record of the same.

(3). In all cases of the ordination under this
Canon of persons with modified requirements
of learning, a record of the modifications shall
be kept by the Bishop, and every Member of the
Clergy thus ordained shall be reported to the
Recorder with the other matters required in
Canon I.1.6(b).

(b). The certificates required in Canon III.7.7(c) and 11(c) shall
be signed by:

(1). Six confirmed adult communicants in good

standing within the Congregation, if there is no
local council of the Congregation;

(2). One Presbyter of the Diocese to whom the
Candidate or Deacon and the community are
personally known, or, in the case of Deacons,
the Presbyter under whose supervision the
Deacon has trained, if there is no Member of the
Clergy in charge of the Congregation.

Sec. 4. In Congregations described in Sec. 1 of this Canon,
where the Sacraments are regularly available, persons described
in Sec. 1(b) may be called by the Bishop and the Congregation
to serve as local Deacons.

(a). The provisions for Postulancy and Candidacy, as set forth
in Sec. 2 of this Canon shall be followed except for Sec. 1(a),
where a certificate shall be as required in Canon III.4.4.(d)(2).

(b). The provisions for ordination as set forth in Canon III.6
shall be followed, except that standards of learning specified in
Canon III.6.4(a) and (b) may be modified as set forth in Sec. 3(a)
of this Canon.

Sec. 5. If a Deacon should be called by a Congregation and the
Bishop to be ordained Priest, the Deacon must meet the requirements as set forth in Secs. 1 and 3 of this Canon.

Sec. 6(a). The Congregations served by persons ordained under
the provisions of this Canon shall be under the supervision of the
Bishop or an appointed deputy.

(b). Under special circumstances, the Bishop may appoint
persons under the provisions of this Canon to serve in more than
one Congregation.

Sec. 7. If Deacons or Priests who have been ordained in accordance with this Canon shall subsequently remove to another

community within the Diocese, they shall be entitled to exercise their office in that place only if:

(a). Requested by the Congregation; and

(b). The Bishop licenses them.

Sec. 8. It is the normal expectation that persons ordained under the provisions of this Canon shall not move from the Congregation and Diocese in which they were ordained. Letters Dimissory may be granted by the Bishop only at the request of the Bishop of the Diocese to which the Deacon or Priest wishes to move.

NOTES

Introduction

1. For a helpful introduction to Roland Allen, see David Paton and Charles H. Long, eds., *A Roland Allen Reader: The Compulsion of the Spirit* (Grand Rapids: Eerdmans, 1983).

2. See William Spofford, "Wesley Frensdorff: The Man and the Mountains," in *Reshaping Ministry: Essays in Memory of Wesley Frensdorff,* ed. Josephine Borgeson and Lynne Wilson (Arvada, Co.: Jethro, 1990).

Chapter 1

1. The forms for such reaffirmation can be found in *The Book of Common Prayer,* in the context of the baptismal or confirmation rites. *The Book of Common Prayer* (New York: Seabury, 1979), see 310 and 419 or, during the Easter Vigil, 292–294.

Chapter 2

1. The *Agreement between the Bishop and Candidate for Ordination as a Local Priest or Deacon* reads as follows:

1. The deacon/priest ordained under the Canons of the Episcopal Church which provide for the ordination of local clergy shall serve only in the congregation which has called him or her to this office and under the supervision of someone appointed for this purpose by the bishop. In other congregations of this Diocese s/he will serve only with the approval of the Bishop and the supervisor, and with the consent of its Vestry/Rector/Regional Vicar.

2. This deacon/priest serves voluntarily without salary or compensation and is not eligible for the Church Pension Fund or diocesan insurance.

3. The deacon/priest shall have a plan for continuing education as outlined in the guidelines. S/he shall make an annual written report to the Bishop and Commission on Ministry on this plan by the First Sunday of Advent.

4. The Bishop and Commission on Ministry shall annually review and affirm the deacon's/priest's functioning in this office, paying particular attention to theological and spiritual growth, as well as the relationship of the deacon/priest with the calling congregation. If such review does not result in approval from the Commission, the Bishop, in consultation with the vestry and Rector/Regional Vicar of the congregation and with the consent of the Standing Committee of the Diocese, may terminate the license to function.

5. The deacon/priest would not wear the traditional clerical collar as ordinary dress, but has the option to do so when performing functions of the office. However, suitable vestments would normally be worn at services as is appropriate and customary in the congregation.

6. When this deacon/priest moves to another parish or diocese, it must be understood that there is no guarantee that those in authority there will grant license to function in this office. When authorities do request such service, the deacon/priest may be

recommended by the Bishop of Nevada, and the past experience in the exercise of the office will be made known.

7. In the event that the calling congregation ceases to exist, this deacon's/priest's license to function is withdrawn.

8. The deacon's/priest's place within the Diocesan Convention is determined by Diocesan Canons.

I understand these conditions and accept them as my responsibilities as a local deacon/priest and hereby commit myself to abide by them.

_____   _____

Candidate   **Date**

Attest:

_____   _____

Bishop   **Date**

2. The Episcopal Diocese of Nevada originally published the *Total Ministry Notebook* in 1981-1982. It was the work of Wes Frensdorff and a few close associates who were involved in the new direction of the Diocese of Nevada. It outlined processes that had worked, especially in the ordination process for local clergy. It included a number of significant theological papers by Bishop Frensdorff.

In 1990, realizing that important changes and growth had taken place, the diocesan commission on ministry undertook the revision of the *Notebook*. Individual members of the commission rewrote or added to the older material, and the commission as a whole met to critique and approve that work. So the *Total Ministry Notebook (1990)* is a community book, reflecting the experience of the community engaged in total-ministry exploration and development. It is a loose-leaf notebook, to be added to and revised on a periodic basis. The latest additions are dated spring 1995.

3. The process for incorporating new, seminary-trained clergy into the diocese is a simple one, involving the following steps:

1. When a calling parish is down to one or two final candidates, those candidates meet with the bishop and then with the local commission on ministry members to discuss the nature of total-ministry development in Nevada.

2. When the new clergyperson has arrived, that person is invited to attend and observe commission on ministry meetings and meetings of the diocesan council and standing committee, to get a firsthand sense of how we work together.

3. Periodic check-in visits with local commission on ministry members are scheduled at six weeks, three months, six months, and one year. The commission members act as a support team for the new clergyperson; they also check in with the vestry of the parish to assure that (1) communications are open, (2) there are no hidden or suppressed problems, and (3) there is appropriate cooperation and affirmation.

4. Without hovering, the bishop stays in touch with the new clergyperson.

Chapter 3

1. Following is the job description for the position of regional vicar for the Diocese of Nevada (revised 1994):

The jobs of the Regional Vicars are diocesan staff positions, focused on the encouragement of ministry in the Diocese of Nevada. Regional Vicars are to be self-starters on one hand, but on the other hand must be team players. They envision these positions to be collegial and to represent the functions expected of the episcopate (bishop). In the Diocese of Nevada they see their jobs as Regional Vicars as an extension of the Bishop's ministry in the areas of ministry development, education, social ministry, and pastoral care and responsibility. They see these as applied concretely in three ways:

Consultation: Regional Vicars are consultants for local congregations in the area of ministry development. They help others to see the bigger picture of mission and ministry in the life of the faith community. They assist parishes with self-evaluation and planning. They also attend functions outside the diocese to share the vision of total ministry within and to learn from the larger church community. Examples are: Other dioceses involved in some total-ministry development, the Western Episcopal Educators Conferences, United Episcopal Charities, C-14, Sindicators, etc.

Education: Regional Vicars assist in the educational needs of parishes and regions, but are not the sole providers of education. They help to plan and coordinate continuing education for parishes and regions. Those who are locally ordained or licensed are required to consult their Regional Vicar annually for their continuing education program. Regional Vicars provide mentoring for local clergy as well as support for any ministers as needed. Examples are: Diocesan School of Theology, offered in the north and the south; classes in specific parishes, according to identified interests and needs; resources for current literature; classes and educational opportunities offered outside the diocese; Preachers-in-Training (PITs) classes, etc.

Linkage: Regional Vicars encourage parishes to interact and cooperate, to share study, to share preachers and the Preachers-in-Training (PITs) classes. They provide linkage to diocesan structures such as the Commission on Ministry, Standing Committee, Diocesan Council, and Diocesan Convention. They also assist in annual goal setting. An important part of linkage has to do with an annual evaluation and accountability with/between Regional Vicars and parishes.

2. Sample Bible study for Nevada diocesan convention focusing on the business of God, sent to parishes in June for study prior to the October convention.

Study Theme:

Mission: Led by the Spirit

Part 1: Confrontation

Text: Luke 4:1-15

Suggestions:

1. Read the passage carefully, several times to yourselves, then aloud in the group. Have a few different translations available.

2. Have someone tell the context of the passage: What was happening as Luke tells the story?

3. Discuss why this passage is pertinent to our story as church in 1994, looking ahead to 2000.

Specific Questions:

1. What is the significance of the Spirit leading Jesus into the wilderness? Doesn't that contradict Luke 11:4b?

2. Is there a general theme or tenor to the temptations? If so, how would you describe it?

3. What do you think makes Jesus so attractive as he emerged from the wilderness? See vv. 14-15. You may also want to compare: Matthew 4:12-17; Mark 1:14-15.

4. What message might this passage have for the church and its structures? Of warning? Of hope?

Part 2: Commitment

Text: Luke 4:16-30

Suggestions as noted above.

Specific questions:

1.   What "amazed" and caused the people in the congregation to speak well of Jesus?

2.   What changed their attitude? Why do you suppose Jesus said what he said in vv. 23-27?

3.   What is the Spirit of the Lord upon Jesus to do?

4.   What might this passage say about the relationship between what people preach and what they practice?

5.   How does this part of the story relate back to the temptations of Jesus?

6.   Reflect on v. 30. What might that say to us as church today and for tomorrow?

Note:

These questions are meant to stimulate thought and reflection. There are no simple answers to them, but they invite us to move more deeply into God's story in order to understand and deepen our responses to God's revelation. The aim is not to find difficulty in the passages, but to live into the story: that we might become more and more a part of it in our own day.

Questions That May Arise from the Bible Study

1.   In both passages, what is the role of the Spirit? How does that relate to other passages that address the role of the Spirit?

2.   In both passages, there seems to be some danger in being led by the Spirit. How does that feel to you as part of a community coordinated by the Spirit (as in 1 Corinthians 12)?

    a.   How does your parish deal with fear as it relates to mission?

    b.   How does your parish respond to opportunity for mission?

    c.   What are some signs that your parish community is coordinated by the Holy Spirit?

    d.   How does that touch and help others?

3.   Where does stewardship fit into this picture? Does the Spirit lead us in the way we use money and time?

4.   What would help us to be more willing *to be led* by the Spirit? In worship? In study? In practice?

5.   Is "our Spirit" better than "theirs"?

6.   How does this speak to your vision of our mission in Nevada as the Episcopal Church in Nevada: people of the Spirit?

How to Help Your Convention Delegates Use This Study

First, assure that your delegates participate fully in your Bible study. Then share with one another the intent of the study as accepted by the diocesan council:

Parish delegations will come to the Convention ready to share some *specific* material about their parish's understanding of mission: in terms of short-term and long-range planning and doing. "Here is one area where the Spirit has led us, and here is what we are doing about that." "It has been hard for us to____." Or, "We are excited at hearing about ___, and that encourages us to____."

It is hoped that, in doing this together, we will deepen our vision of how we relate to one another as parishes that are diocese, and how the Spirit may be working among us to encourage our mission in the name of Jesus Christ.

The Alban Institute:
an invitation to membership

The Alban Institute, begun in 1974, believes that the congregation is essential to the task of equipping the people of God to minister in the church and the world. A multi-denominational membership organization, the Institute provides on-site training, educational programs, consulting, research, and publishing for hundreds of churches across the country.

The Alban Institute invites you to be a member of this partnership of laity, clergy, and executives–a partnership that brings together people who are raising important questions about congregational life and people who are trying new solutions, making new discoveries, finding a new way of getting clear about the task of ministry. The Institute exists to provide you with the kinds of information and resources you need to support your ministries.

Join us now and enjoy these benefits:

CONGREGATIONS: The Alban Journal, a highly respected journal published six times a year, to keep you up to date on current issues and trends.

Inside Information, Alban's quarterly newsletter, keeps you informed about research and other happenings around Alban. Available to members only.

Publications Discounts:

- ☐ 15% for Individual, Retired Clergy, and Seminarian Members
- ☐ 25% for Congregational Members
- ☐ 40% for Judicatory and Seminary Executive Members

Discounts on Training and Education Events

Write our Membership Department at the address below or call us at 1-800-486-1318 or 301-718-4407 for more information about how to join The Alban Institute's growing membership, particularly about Congregational Membership in which 12 designated persons receive all benefits of membership.

**The Alban Institute, Inc.
Suite 433 North
4550 Montgomery Avenue
Bethesda, MD 20814-3341**